Teaching Our Children to Think

John Langrehr

National Educational Service
Bloomington, Indiana

Copyright © 2001 by National Educational Service
304 West Kirkwood Avenue
Bloomington, IN 47404-5147
(812) 336-7700
(800) 733-6786 (toll free)
FAX: (812) 336-7790
e-mail: nes@nesonline.com
www.nesonline.com

Cover art and design by Grannan Graphic Design Ltd.

Text Design by T.G. Design Group

Art by Joe Lee

Printed in the United States of America

ISBN 1-879639-76-9

TABLE OF CONTENTS

PREFACE

A NEW WAY OF THINKING

Thinking often involves asking our brains to remember information we have stored in our memories. This type of thinking—memorization—has become so common that school programs have been dominated by the teaching of content to remember and the testing of this information to see how well it has been remembered. Because we obviously need information to think about, this kind of thinking will always be important. However, today we have so much new information to think about, and so many electronic devices and networks to help us find and retrieve it, that we also need to be good at other kinds of thinking, such as creative and critical thinking.

These other ways of thinking that have been neglected in school programs involve students asking themselves questions about information they have remembered. Self-questioning is essential for making physical connections between new and stored information in our brains. The fewer the questions we ask about information, the fewer the connections we make in our brains. Luckily, self-questioning is something that can be taught and learned. Self-questioning is the essential requirement for understanding information and for thinking analytically, critically, and creatively about it.

PROCESSING PROGRAMS OF THE BRAIN

Computer processing programs, such as those we use for spelling, statistics, and calculating, consist of a series of short questions that are fed into the main memory of a computer. Human information processing programs in our brains also consist of a series of short questions. We rapidly and unconsciously ask ourselves these questions when we think in different ways. For example, we have one group of questions that we ask ourselves when we try to decide whether a statement is a fact or an opinion. We have another group of questions for trying to remember the spelling of a difficult word, and yet another for distinguishing relevant from irrelevant factors. The quantity and quality of questions that make up each of our thinking programs varies widely from person to person. People who find it difficult to distinguish facts from opinions have very few relevant questions in their processing programs for this basic **thinking process**. And people who are poor spellers have never been taught some relevant questions to ask themselves when trying to remember the spelling of a new word. For example:

1. How many syllables or small words are in this word?
2. What does the word start and end with?
3. Are there any parts in the word that might be difficult to remember?
4. Do any parts sound unlike the way they are spelled?
5. What does the word mean?
6. Does this word look like any other word that I know?
7. Can I picture this word in some way?

In short, people who are poor spellers may never have been taught **how** to spell!

CORE THINKING PROCESSES

Of course, students cannot learn groups of questions to ask themselves for every physical and mental process they use. However, they can learn them for the basic or core thinking processes that they are likely to use every day. It is estimated that we use 20 to 30 core thinking processes each day for processing information that we sense. These processes have been identified and described in *Dimensions of Thinking* (Marzano, 1988). Students can never learn how to think effectively if they do not have a range of questions for handling these core thinking processes. Although some students learn these questions naturally, most students need to be taught these processing questions. Helping students understand and apply these questions to their own thinking is a major aim of this book.

Core Thinking Processes* and Related Exercises

Thinking Process	Exercises in This Book That Test and Develop the Process
Focusing Skills	
1. Defining problems	Exercise 22: Making a decision
2. Setting goals	Exercise 22: Making a decision
Information–Gathering Skills	
3. Observing	Exercise 1: Observing properties
4. Formulating questions	Exercise 25: Asking your own questions
Remembering Skills	
5. Encoding	
6. Recalling	Content themes, section II
Organizing Skills	
7. Comparing	Exercise 2: Observing similarities Exercise 3: Observing differences Exercise 6: Comparing
8. Classifying	Exercise 4: Categorizing similar things Exercise 5: Identifying non-examples of a category Exercise 7: Sorting things into categories
9. Ordering	Exercise 8: Organizing things in order of size Exercise 9: Organizing things in order of time

*From *Dimensions of Thinking* (Marzano, 1988).

(continued)

Evaluating Skills

20. Establishing criteria   Exercise 20: Distinguishing relevant from
                                       irrelevant information
                                    Exercise 22: Making a decision

21. Verifying   Exercise 19: Challenging the reliability of
                                       a claim
                                    Exercise 21: Thinking critically about
                                       what you read
                                    Exercise 24: Considering other points of
                                       view

Unfortunately, many teachers and parents **assume** that students naturally learn—without instruction—a range of useful questions for processing information. This is strange because we do not assume that students naturally learn content without instruction. In other words, many people demand that teachers teach students **what** to think about, but not **how** to think about it! Students often find it difficult to think in certain ways simply because they do not know the processing questions to ask themselves.

METACOGNITION

How can students learn better processing questions for the various core thinking processes? The answer lies in the use of metacognition, a process that research shows to be the most powerful factor in improving student thinking and learning (Wang, 1994). **Metacognition** involves a learner carefully reflecting on and sharing the specific thoughts that pass through his or her mind while doing a mental or physical task. Listening to or looking up the correct answers to questions is not enough to improve thinking. Students have to be allowed "inside the minds" of others who are good at spelling, problem solving, reading critically, designing, and so on, as they do specific tasks associated with these ways of thinking. Once inside, all students can observe and learn from the patterns good thinkers sense, the questions they ask themselves, and the mental images they use to clarify and summarize incoming information.

This book, *Teaching Our Children to Think,* can help all students think more effectively because it provides them with questions that engage a wide range of core thinking processes. But it is only part of what they need. Metacognition must also be present if poor thinkers are to learn the thinking questions that good thinkers use. Some examples of these questions used for core thinking processes are provided in Appendix A.

POSITIVE THOUGHTS FOR GOOD THINKING

Of course, students will improve their thinking only if they want to. They also have to believe that they can. They have to have the self-esteem, confidence, persistence, and motivation to give it a try. Some students will need work on their **emotional intelligence** as well as their **processing intelligence**. Students can improve **thinking skills** by learning better questions with which to process information. They can improve **emotional skills** by learning **positive thoughts** to repeat to themselves when they are trying to learn new tasks. Some examples of such positive thoughts are included in Appendix B.

WHAT ARE THE QUESTIONS IN THIS BOOK ABOUT?

The book is divided into three sections. Section I has questions that engage many of the **core thinking processes** identified by educators over the years. The content in these questions includes **language arts, social studies, science,** and **mathematics.** Section II of the book contains questions related to a range of **high-interest topics.** The type of thinking process being challenged by each question is clearly shown.

The questions in section II test whether students can **transfer** the thinking processes developed in section I to a range of different content areas. These content areas include animals, plants, weather, energy, pollution, and polygons, among others.

Section III contains four appendix sections, including a summary of the key thinking processes, an overview of helpful positive thoughts, possible answers to the exercises, and a list of references and resources.

WHAT ABOUT THE ANSWERS TO THE QUESTIONS?

The **suggested answers** to the questions in each exercise are provided in Appendix C. I say "suggested" because questions that involve creative and critical thinking usually have more than one correct answer. Such is the nature of higher-order thinking. You and your students may have other correct answers. Always allow a student to defend his or her answer. If you don't, you won't be encouraging independent, critical, and creative thinking.

WHO IS THE BOOK FOR?

Most students in grades 6 to 10 will be successful with the majority of the questions in each exercise. **Gifted students** will enjoy the exercises because many of the questions allow for a variety of complex and creative answers. Other students will also find success because they can come up with acceptable answers depending on their content knowledge. **Teachers** will also find the book useful because the questions provide **models** for designing thought-producing questions on other topics. And **parents and grandparents** will find the book useful if they want to help a child or grandchild develop core thinking processes outside of school.

HOW DO YOU USE THE BOOK?

Exercises modeled after the exercises in this book can be given to students in a **weekly lesson** as part of a **social studies** or **self-development** course. The book could form the basis of a separate **short course** aimed at developing thinking processes. The book would also make a useful **library resource** for students who seek a mental challenge. In other words, it is a book for those students who may no longer be challenged by the usual correct answers or questions that test memory.

After completing each exercise in section 1, it is vital for the reader to summarize and write down any useful questions he or she asked to complete the questions in the exercises. These can be compared with the questions suggested in Appendix A. These groups of questions for the core thinking processes become the reader's "thinking chips" for future use.

If you are a parent using the book at home, it is important to discuss with your child the introductions to the sections and to the individual exercises. Question your child to check his or her understanding of the introduction. Clarify the meaning of the instructions for each exercise. Work together through the first question or two of each exercise. Think aloud the thoughts you had in coming up with your answers to these questions. Remember that metacognition is a powerful factor in learning and new thinking.

The ideal approach, however, is to **integrate** questions (Swartz & Parks, 1994) that challenge the core thinking processes into regular curriculum content. Teaching thinking processes in a separate course may not be the best strategy, but it is often the most realistic. Teachers are very busy and often do not have the time to design groups of questions like those in the second section of this book. One of my goals in writing this book was to save teachers some time by providing them with model questions to use in designing better questions. After all, **better questions** are needed for **better student thinking**.

A FINAL WORD

The exercises in this book are not just chosen at random. The thinking processes involved are based on the research of hundreds of educators working at all levels of education. These include national leaders of teams of researchers such as Resnick (1989), Perkins (1992), and Paul (1992). They are sequenced here in roughly the order in which we learn them from our first observations of the world around us.

The questions in the following exercises require the reader to do more than recall a correct answer that has been memorized. Instead, the questions engage the reader's processing intelligence and content intelligence.

Thinking can be fun if you have the tools to think with. It is my hope that this book will provide your children and students with these tools.

—John Langrehr

THINKING PROCESSES

CHAPTER 1

PRETESTS OF CREATIVE AND CRITICAL THINKING

Creative and critical thinking are vital in today's world of rapid change, competition, and information that constantly demands judgment. Most people find creative and critical thinking difficult because these forms of thinking are rarely taught in school. It is assumed that students learn how to think in these ways without instruction.

Before you begin working through the exercises in this book, you might like to test your creative and critical thinking skills. Your answers to the following questions will give you an idea of the level of your creative and critical thinking abilities. Some suggested answers for the tests are given in Appendix C. The questions in the following two pretests introduce you to many of the core thinking processes discussed in this book. They also provide a preview of the kinds of exercises in this book that will help you develop your creative and critical thinking skills. A score of 20 or more for either test indicates that you are already a very good creative and/or critical thinker. Even if you score more than 20 for either test, the challenging exercises in this book will help you improve your skills because the exercises cover a wide variety of subjects and require many other core thinking processes that are not covered in the tests.

THE LANGREHR PRETEST OF CREATIVE THINKING (GRADES SIX AND UP)

This test is suitable for students in grades six and up. It should be completed within 40 minutes; 24 points are possible. No prompting should be needed.

1. List four things that you COULD NOT photograph. (4 points)

    a. _____   c. _____
    b. _____   d. _____

2. List four ways in which a tree and a car are the SAME. (4 points)

    a. _____   c. _____
    b. _____   d. _____

3. List three possible REASONS why a man might be observed reading a newspaper in the park with the paper UPSIDE DOWN. (3 points)

    a. _____   c. _____
    b. _____

4. List four VERY DIFFERENT USES for a brick, other than to build a wall. (4 points)

    a. _____   c. _____
    b. _____   d. _____

5. List three ways of getting a Ping-Pong ball out of a narrow steel pipe that is 3 feet long and whose base is stuck in concrete. You CAN'T DAMAGE the pipe, the concrete, or the ball. (3 points)

    a. _____   c. _____
    b. _____

6. List two VERY DIFFERENT THINGS the following line drawing could represent. (2 points)

    a. _____

    b. _____

7. Put your pencil on dot A. Now, without taking your pencil from the paper, join these nine dots using NO MORE THAN FOUR straight lines, continuously connected. (2 points)

    A

8. Imagine that you are in a prison cell with only the morning NEWSPAPER, some RUBBER BANDS, a HAMMER, and a CUSHION. There is a narrow bottle in the hallway outside the cell. The bottle is 3 yards away from the open bars of the cell door. If you can place the round marble that you have in your pocket into this bottle, you will be released. Write down how you would do this. (2 points)

    Method:

    _____
    _____
    _____

THE LANGREHR PRETEST OF CRITICAL THINKING (GRADES SIX AND UP)

This test is suitable for students in grades six and up. It should be completed within 40 minutes; 25 points are possible. No prompting should be needed.

1. Complete the following statement so that the last two things are related in the SAME way as the first two things. (1 point)

    Book is to rectangle as coin is to _____.

2. Circle the letters in front of the two FACTS. The other sentences are opinions. (2 points)

    a. Animals are more useful to humans than plants.

    b. There were more people in the world in 2000 than there were in 1999.

    c. The president of the United States should always be a man.

    d. Animals and trees both need air to live.

    e. Women are better doctors than men.

3. In the following story, one of the events CAUSED one of the other events to happen. Circle the letter in front of the CAUSE and underline the letter in front of the EFFECT. (2 points)

    a. Tom went fishing in his boat.

    b. There was a rainbow in the sky.

    c. He was worried about the rough waves.

    d. He could see a large ship on the horizon.

    e. Out at sea, the sun shone on the misty rain.

4. Imagine that you lost your dog. Circle the letters in front of the three MOST IMPORTANT things about your dog that you think would help people find it. (3 points)

    a. Where you got the dog.

    b. How fast the dog can run.

    c. The color of the dog.

    d. The name of the dog.

    e. The breed of the dog.

    f. What the dog eats.

    g. Where the dog sleeps.

    h. The name of the dog next door.

5. After each sentence, write what you think the thing in CAPITAL LETTERS is. (3 points)

    a. The RAPTOR swept down from the cliff and killed the mouse. _____

    b. The men pulled the SEINE around the school of fish.
        _____

    c. The girl climbed the COQUITO as it gently swayed in the breeze. _____

6. Underline the three words in the following advertisement whose exact meanings are NOT CLEAR to the reader. These words might trick some people. The ad was placed by used car dealer Fred Smith, who is having a sale this weekend. (3 points)

    Every car will be sold at half price. If you buy a car from Fred Smith, you know it is guaranteed.

(continued)

7.   In a newspaper report, a man claims to have seen a large, glowing unidentified flying object (UFO) hovering over the ocean in front of his house. Which three of these facts would help you, or anyone else, BELIEVE that his report could be true? Circle the letter in front of the three facts you choose. (3 points)

a.   The ocean was rough.

b.   He saw it for 10 minutes.

c.   There was a new moon.

d.   It was exactly 10 P.M.

e.   He saw it with binoculars.

f.   Friends next door saw it.

g.   The man was 25 years old.

8.   On Monday, Helen finds out that all of the goldfish in the class aquarium have died. Circle the letters in front of the three MOST USEFUL pieces of evidence that should help her discover HOW they died. (3 points)

a.   There are no marks on the fish.

b.   The fish were a pretty color.

c.   It was raining over the weekend.

d.   Food is floating on the water.

e.   The fish are floating on top of the water.

f.   Air bubbles are coming from the aerator.

9.   Nancy noticed the light was on in the kitchen of the house next door at 3 o'clock in the morning. Write two things she CAN BE SURE OF and two things she CAN'T BE SURE OF. (2 points)

Can be sure of:

a.   _____

b.   _____

Can't be sure of:

a.   _____

b.   _____

10. Draw a circle around the letters of the three things YOU CAN'T BE SURE OF in the following picture. (3 points)

a. The boy is holding a baseball bat.

b. The boy is a good baseball player.

c. The woman is standing up.

d. The man is sitting down.

e. The boy is the son of the man.

f. The man is holding a football.

g. The man is sad that the boy is not playing football.

CHAPTER 2

EXERCISES TO IMPROVE MENTAL ORGANIZATION

When you ask your brain to think about something, it has to search among the words, pictures, ideas, facts, and other things it has stored in its memory. It is like looking for a page in a file, when that file is hidden in a filing cabinet. The messier or more disorganized your filing cabinet is, the more difficult it is to find the file and the page that you are looking for. This is also true with your brain—your "**mental filing cabinet.**"

Your mental filing cabinet is full of files of content to think with and files of questions to ask yourself about this content. The more **organized** the contents and questions are in your brain, the quicker and more efficient you will be in finding the information in your memory that you want to think with.

Isn't it amazing that your brain uses **criteria,** or properties, to **file** new examples of things you notice and learn into small "**boxes**" in your memory? For example, you have boxes for red things, countries, verbs, metals, expensive things, and so on. Some of your boxes have many examples in them, depending on how much you have read, what you have listened to in class, and also on what you are really interested in and good at. You have even connected some boxes to each other to help you remember things that share characteristics, such as things that are both red and made of metal.

To be a **good thinker**, you first have to be good at noticing and remembering the properties, or features, of what is around you. You have to do more than just look. You have to **notice** that a tree is tall, vertical, alive, and made of wood, and that it needs air, water, and sunlight to live. You also have to **ask yourself** useful **questions** about what you are looking at. What does a verb look like? How can I recognize a metal? What do all countries have? The more properties you notice and the more questions you ask yourself about these properties, the stronger your potential to become a better thinker.

Exercises 1 through 12 will help you to learn some useful properties and questions you can use to sort and organize things in your mental filing cabinet.

1. OBSERVING PROPERTIES

Why is a pencil made of wood? And why does it usually have six sides? Everything around us has special features, or properties. There are reasons for these properties. But you will never know the reasons unless you ask **why**. To be a good thinker, you need to be a thoughtful observer. This exercise will make you think about some of the same questions that passed through the minds of the first people to create a pencil, brick, coin, flag, and car tire. I hope you will try this exercise with many more of the things around you.

Instructions

Write three properties that you have noticed for each of the following things. After each property, write a reason why you think the thing has this property.

THING	PROPERTIES	REASON FOR PROPERTY
1. brick	• rough	• cement sticks easily to surface
	• heavy	• wind won't blow it away
	• rectangular	• easy to stack together in lines

2. coin   _____   _____

                     _____   _____

                     _____   _____

3. flag   _____   _____

                     _____   _____

                     _____   _____

4. car tire   _____   _____

                     _____   _____

                     _____   _____

5. bottle   _____   _____

                     _____   _____

                     _____   _____

6. football   _____   _____

                     _____   _____

                     _____   _____

7. newspaper _____   _____

                     _____   _____

                     _____   _____

2. OBSERVING SIMILARITIES

Have you ever thought about how pairs of things are similar? How could a tree be similar to an ant? You haven't been taught how they could be similar. However, if you have organized and stored some properties of ants and trees in your mind, you will find some properties that they have in common. The questions in this exercise will help you make many unusual connections between things.

Instructions

Write three or more ways in which the first thing in each pair is the SAME as the second thing in the pair.

THINGS

1. banana and lemon

2. triangle and square

3. ant and tree

4. the numbers 4 and 9

5. team and family

6. the words *fell* and *ran*

SIMILAR PROPERTIES

- yellow
- food
- thick skins
- grow on trees

3. OBSERVING DIFFERENCES

It is also useful to notice how things are different from each other. For example, a cat and a dog may be similar in that they are both living, both animals, both have four legs, or both eat meat. However, only a cat can meow or climb trees. This exercise tests whether or not you have noticed and stored small differences between things.

Instructions

Write three or more ways in which the first item in each pair is DIFFERENT FROM the second item.

THINGS

DIFFERENT PROPERTIES

1. cat and dog
- cat can climb trees
- meows
- chases mice

2. crab and fish

3. circle and triangle

4. lake and ocean

5. the numbers 4 and 11

6. newspaper and book

7. bird and bee

8. artery and vein

9. verbs and nouns

10. president and queen

11. democracy and
    dictatorship

12. the numbers 25 and 26

4. CATEGORIZING SIMILAR THINGS

This exercise is more difficult than exercise 2 because you have to find a property that is common to three things rather than two things. It will really test how good the connections are that link similar things together in your memory.

Instructions

The three things in the following groups are the SAME in some way. How are they the same?

THINGS

1. scissors, magnet, nail
2. ant, beetle, butterfly
3. light, heat, sound
4. ice, fog, steam
5. push, friction, gravity
6. rabbit, deer, cow
7. coal, sunlight, uranium
8. lever, ramp, pulley
9. snake, alligator, lizard
10. hydrogen, oxygen, iron
11. echo, music, thunder
12. election, vote, senator
13. eating, sleeping, drinking
14. cotton, wool, hemp
15. photograph, page, door
16. tire, coin, cog
17. cork, iceberg, apple
18. photosynthesis, shadows, photoelectricity
19. the numbers 7, 11, and 13
20. the numbers 16, 64, and 36

REASONS THEY ARE THE SAME

1. made of metal, machine-made

21. triangle, square, pentagon _____

22. the words *walk, catch,* and *climb* _____

5. IDENTIFYING NON–EXAMPLES OF A CATEGORY

This exercise is more difficult than exercise 3. Here you have to find ONE THING that is DIFFERENT from three other things. There will be more than one correct answer, but you have to indicate WHY you chose yours. For example, in item 1 only a horse can be ridden, or only a dog eats meat. Both answers are correct.

Instructions

Which ONE thing in the following groups is DIFFERENT from the other three things in some way? Write it and explain your reasoning.

GROUPS   DIFFERENT THING

1. cow, horse, dog, goat   dog

WHY? Because it eats meat; is allowed inside.

2. orange, grapefruit, pear, lemon

_____

3. wood, plastic, cotton, rubber

_____

4. sphere, cube, rectangle, cylinder

_____

5. went, smiles, climbed, sat

_____

6. parallelogram, square, octagon, rectangle

_____

7. degrees, graphs, grams, seconds

_____

8. Mars, Earth, Moon, Venus

_____

9. peninsula, gulf, cape, island

_____

10. fish, snake, bird, worm

_____

11. president, king, mayor, governor

_____

12. oil, timber, natural gas, coal

_____

13. the numbers 12, 27, 25, and 39

_____

14. the numbers 25, 16, 21, and 36

_____

15. Circle the different item:

16. Circle the different item:

17. the words *run, rag, rat,* and *ram*

_____

18. the words *run, hit, slow,* and *fall*

_____

19. oak, pine, maple, ash

_____

20. nylon, wax, polyester, Teflon™

_____

21. skin, vein, hair, nail

_____

22. rat, guinea pig, mouse, anteater

_____

23. frost, cloud, dust, dew

_____

24. heat, gas, sound, light

_____

25. moon, sun, lamp, fire

_____

26. electron, crystal, neutron, proton

_____

27. oxygen, nitrogen, carbon dioxide, hydrogen sulfide

_____

28. stomach, mouth, lungs, intestine

_____

6. COMPARING

In this exercise, you have to think about how two things are DIFFERENT and how they are the SAME. It might help you to think about the size, color, use, material, parts, and shape of the two things you are comparing. Remember the acronym formed from the first letters of these properties: SCUMPS.

Instructions

Write three ways in which the following pairs of things are the SAME and three ways in which they are DIFFERENT.

Trees/Insects

Only Trees	Both	Only Insects
1. are made of wood	need air	have a head and eyes
2. _____	_____	_____
3. _____	_____	_____

Dinosaurs/Elephants

Only Dinosaurs	Both	Only Elephants
1. _____	_____	_____
2. _____	_____	_____
3. _____	_____	_____

Books/Newspapers

Only Books	Both	Only Newspapers
1. _____	_____	_____
2. _____	_____	_____
3. _____	_____	_____

Snails/Crabs

Only Snails	Both	Only Crabs
1. _____	_____	_____
2. _____	_____	_____
3. _____	_____	_____

Chess/Football

Only Chess	Both	Only Football
1. _____	_____	_____
2. _____	_____	_____
3. _____	_____	_____

Moon/Earth

Only the Moon	Both	Only the Earth
1. _____	_____	_____
2. _____	_____	_____
3. _____	_____	_____

7. SORTING THINGS INTO CATEGORIES

Here is an exercise that really makes you search for the connections in your memory. This time, the names of three categories, or groups of things, are given. You have to sort the individual items into these groups. Some items may belong to more than one category.

Instructions

Place the things in each list into one of the three specified groups.

1. FOOD: milk, carrots, cheese, apples, melons, potatoes, butter, cream, pears, berries, onions, bananas

Fruits	Vegetables	Dairy Foods
apples	onions	butter
berries	carrots	cheese
_____	_____	_____
_____	_____	_____

2. TOOLS: spade, plane, rake, saw, file, sander, chisel, hammer, shovel, mallet, sledgehammer

For the Garden	For Hitting and Pounding	For Cutting and Smoothing

3. MATH CONCEPTS: rectangle, foot, cylinder, cube, mile, triangle, pyramid, square, kilometer, pentagon, sphere

Two–Dimensional	Three–Dimensional

4. BODY PARTS: intestine, kidney, bladder, nose, stomach, lungs, windpipe, saliva, sweat glands, mouth

Digestive	Excretory	Respiratory

5. HUMAN LIFE: food, joy, car, water, holidays, sleep, jewelry, hate, jealousy

Needs	Wants	Emotions

6. OCCUPATIONS: journalist, lawyer, judge, cartoonist, salesperson, actor, prison officer, sheriff, manager, photographer

Media	Law	Business
_____	_____	_____
_____	_____	_____
_____	_____	_____
_____	_____	_____

7. BIRDS: condor, ostrich, gull, eagle, swan, owl, emu, kiwi, flamingo, pelican, hawk

Of Prey	Water	Flightless
_____	_____	_____
_____	_____	_____
_____	_____	_____
_____	_____	_____

8. SUBSTANCES: steel, water, air, plastic, oxygen, alcohol, carbon dioxide, wood, copper, kerosene, nitrogen, oil

Solid	Liquid	Gas
_____	_____	_____
_____	_____	_____
_____	_____	_____
_____	_____	_____

8. ORGANIZING THINGS IN ORDER OF SIZE

In our brains we also organize things in an order, or sequence. For example, we order things in terms of their size, speed, cost, and so on. Ordering and comparing things is all part of connecting them in our memories in an organized way.

Instructions

The following related things are placed out of order. Rewrite them in order of their SIZE, starting with the largest.

THINGS	ORDERED BY DECREASING SIZE
1. sentence, paragraph word	paragraph, sentence, word
2. lane, path, highway, road	
3. forest, branch, tree, twig	
4. speech, act, scene, play	
5. artery, circulatory system, body, heart	
6. planet, universe, moon, sun	
7. reflex angle, acute angle, obtuse angle, right angle	

8. retina, eye, rod,
   sensory system

   _____

   _____

9. crystal, molecule,
   atom, nucleus

   _____

   _____

10. nation, community,
    family, daughter

    _____

    _____

11. senator, government,
    party, nation

    _____

    _____

12. Catholic, priest, culture,
    religion

    _____

    _____

13. city, suburb, country,
    state

    _____

    _____

14. inch, yard, foot, mile

    _____

    _____

9. ORGANIZING THINGS IN ORDER OF TIME

As you have just seen, we often order things in terms of their size—sometimes without even being told to do so. We also order things in terms of time, or when they happen in a sequence. You will order unorganized items in the following exercise.

Instructions

The following things are placed out of order. Rewrite them in order of the TIME in which they occur. Start with the FIRST THING in the sequence.

THINGS	ORDERED BY TIME (FIRST TO LAST)
1. dusk, midday, dawn, midnight	dawn, midday, dusk, midnight
2. thunder, flood, lightning, rain	
3. caterpillar, egg, butterfly	
4. car, hovercraft, plane, bicycle	
5. clock, sundial, sun, watch	
6. election, nomination, campaign	
7. invent, sell, manufacture, research	
8. compose, rehearse, perform	
9. mill, harvest, bake, eat	
10. landscape, design, paint, build	

10. GENERALIZING ABOUT EXAMPLES

Think of all the birds you have seen in books or in real life. Do they have anything in common? It depends on how many you have seen. Somewhere in your brain you have a picture of a bird with feathers, a beak, eggs, a nest, in flight, and so on. This is your generalization of a bird.

Why do we generalize? It helps us to recognize new examples of birds, and it helps us to predict what a new bird that we observe might be able to do. You also have mental pictures of cars, chairs, triangles, and many other things.

Instructions

In the following exercises, you will examine your generalizations about certain items.

1. Write down four or more properties that are COMMON TO ALL coins that you know of. These are your generalizations about coins.

    ALL COINS:
    a. are metal   c._____
    b. have a date   d._____

2. Write down four or more properties or features that are COMMON TO ALL stamps that you know of. These are your generalizations about stamps.

    ALL STAMPS:
    a._____   c._____
    b._____   d._____

3. Write down four or more properties that are COMMON TO ALL English words. These are your generalizations about words.

    ALL WORDS:
    a._____   c._____
    b._____   d._____

4. Look at the following examples of polygons. Write down as many properties as you can that are COMMON TO ALL of these polygons. These are your generalizations about polygons.

ALL POLYGONS:

_____

_____

_____

_____

5. Write down 5 to 10 examples of sports in the space below. Examples:

_____

_____

_____

_____

Now write down as many properties, or features, of these sports as you can. When you have done this, cross out any features that ARE NOT COMMON to all of the examples you gave. The features left are your generalizations about all sports. Features:

_____

_____

_____

_____

6. Write down 5 to 10 examples of methods of transport in the space below.
   Examples:

   _____

   _____

   _____

   _____

   Now write down as many properties, or features, of these methods of transport as possible. When you have done this, cross out any features that ARE NOT COMMON to all of the examples you gave. The features left are your generalizations about all methods of transport.
   Features:

   _____

   _____

   _____

   _____

Instructions

In questions 7 through 9, write "yes" if the example given contains the property at the top of the columns. Write "no" if it doesn't contain the property. Which properties do ALL of the examples have in common?

7. Some Properties of Mammals

Mammals	Properties					
	Legs	Back-bone	Lungs	Warm-Blooded	Can Swim	Can Fly
Humans						
Whales						
Dogs						
Bats						

Generalization: All mammals

_____

_____

8. Some Properties of Metals

Metals	Properties			
	Conducts Electricity	Is Solid	Is Magnetic	Melts Easily
Iron				
Aluminum				
Tin				
Mercury				

Generalization: All metals

_____

_____

9. Some Properties of Insects

Insects	Properties				
	Six Legs	Body Segments	Antennae	Wings	Eyes
Grasshopper					
Beetle					
Fly					
Ant					
Bee					

Generalization: All insects

_____

_____

10. What generalization can you make about high fiber foods from the following facts?

Food	Properties		
	Low Fat	Low Sugar	High Fiber
Lettuce	yes	yes	yes
Cheese	no	yes	no
Apples	yes	yes	yes
Baked Beans	yes	yes	yes
Cake	no	no	no

Generalization: High-fiber foods

_____

_____

11. VERBAL SUMMARIZING

The first part of summarizing a reading is identifying the **main topic,** or main idea. As you read, look for important words or repeated words and one **main sentence** that tells what the reading is all about. Once you think you know what the main idea is, look for other sentences that give you **relevant** or **useful** information about this topic. A summary of these sentences should be in your final summary.

Instructions

In each of the following readings:

1. Make up a title with fewer than eight words that tells what the reading is about.

2. Underline one sentence that you think is the main sentence.

3. Circle two sentences that you think are very important to consider in creating a summary because they contain a lot of relevant information about the topic.

4. Write a summary of no more than 30 words.

READING 1

Your Title: _____

Their shining surfaces are the playgrounds of millions of people; their dim bottoms are the resting places of thousands of wrecks. They serve two nations in many ways: cooling cities, quenching thirsts, carrying away sewage, generating electricity, fending off tornadoes, and providing ocean ports a thousand miles inland. Sometimes they remind us that they were not placed on the earth to be our servants. With eroding waves, they devour beaches and summer cottages. Of course we are talking about the Great Lakes. These lakes cover nearly 25,000 square miles of North America, making them the greatest expanse of fresh water on this planet. Even the smallest of them, Lake Ontario, ranks 14th among the world's lakes. I am amazed at the injury humans have done to the lakes, and by the urgent task that we now face in keeping the lakes alive. The Great Lakes play an important role as weather makers. Lake Superior is second in area to the Caspian Sea, which is also a lake because it is surrounded by land.

(Adapted from *National Geographic,* August 1973, p. 147–150.)

Write your summary (maximum length 30 words):

_____

_____

_____

READING 2

Your Title: _____

It was an unusual fishing party because we were trying to catch something too small to see. All three of us were dressed for icy weather. A half-hour later, I looked through the microscope to see some algae. Algae are among the most widespread and hardiest of living things. They grow in ice and snow, hot springs, and even salty seas. Without algae, it is doubtful that humans could have evolved and survived. Perhaps as much as 90% of all photo-synthesis is done by algae. Photosynthesis produces oxygen.

The lake we were on was about 30 miles from Manhattan. We took samples from the lake at about 150 yards from the shore. There are about 30,000 species of algae, ranging from one-celled organisms to seaweed such as giant kelp. Algae are wonderful eaters of pollutants in our rivers and lakes.

(Adapted from *National Geographic,* March 1974, p. 361.)

Write your summary (maximum length 30 words):

_____

_____

_____

12. VISUAL SUMMARIZING

One good picture summary can save you from writing hundreds of words. Picture summaries simplify and clarify the main points of a reading. In this way, they help you to think clearly. The process of visual summarizing involves identifying the main terms or words in a reading, and then writing them on a picture or map. Different-shaped maps are available, so it is wise to choose a map whose shape matches the shape of the ideas in your reading.

A simple way to visually show relationships is to use a table format to compare and contrast two items.

1.

Only Books	Both	Only Newspapers
a. _____	_____	_____
b. _____	_____	_____
c. _____	_____	_____

More complex ways to understand relationships are shown in the next two exercises.

Instructions

Fill in the missing word or words where there are question marks on the following visual maps. Notice the shapes of the maps. Why are they good shapes to use in summarizing the information they contain? Notice how they give a quick, clear summary to any reader.

2. TREES

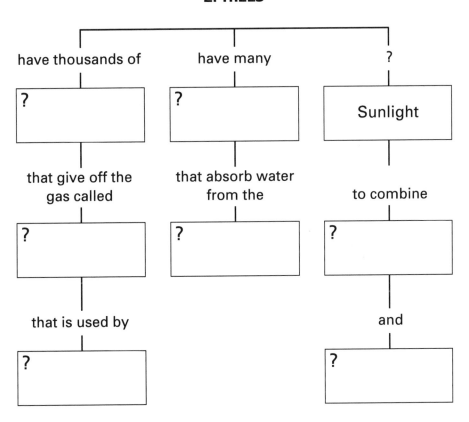

(continued)

3. BUTTERFLIES

that break open to
release

lay many

?

?

that get a hard shell
around them to form

that hatch
to form

?

CHAPTER 3

EXERCISES TO IMPROVE ANALYTICAL THINKING

Exercises 1 through 12 helped you to organize things better in your mental filing cabinet. Exercises 13 through 16 will help you do more than think about whole things—you will think about their **parts** and how they are **related**, or connected, to each other. This is called **analytical thinking**.

Two things can be related to each other because they have the same use, color, shape, material, and so on. You learned this in exercise 6. In exercises 8 and 9, you learned how you sometimes store things in your brain in an order or sequence. For example, we often store things in our mental filing cabinet by size or time. In exercise 14, you will see how we often order things in terms of their parts. You have to analyze, or figure out, how the parts are changing in a sequence.

Analytical thinking is more than just organizing things in your brain. It is like being a mental detective—you have to figure out certain features and then use these features to solve a problem.

13. ANALYZING RELATIONSHIPS

The type of question in this exercise is often found in intelligence tests. Good thinkers are quick to analyze the relationship between smaller things and the larger thing that they are part of.

Instructions

How is the first thing related to the second thing in each of the following statements? Identify the missing thing that would be related in the same way to the third thing, and write it in the blank. In example one, the missing thing should relate to "fish" in the same way that "bird" relates to "feathers." Feathers cover the body of a bird. What covers the body of a fish? The answer is "scales."

1. bird is to feathers as fish is to <u>scales</u>.

2. blue is to color as eagle is to _____.

3. Sun is to star as Earth is to _____.

4. stomach is to food as lungs are to _____.

5. triangle is to three as square is to _____.

6. circle is to sphere as square is to _____.

7. artist is to studio as judge is to _____.

8. 3 is to 5 as 60 is to _____.

9. link is to chain as word is to _____.

10. oak is to deciduous as pine is to _____.

11. Moon is to planet as electron is to _____.

12. artery is to blood as nerve is to _____.

13. president is to nation as mayor is to _____.

14. retina is to eye as ventricle is to _____.

15. Chinese is to Asian as Catholic is to _____.

16. heat is to energy as push is to _____.

17. *sing* is to *sang* as *ride* is to _____.

18. *went* is to verb as *dog* is to _____.

19. oxygen is to element as salt is to _____.

Now make up some of your own!

14. ANALYZING PATTERNS IN A SEQUENCE

Here is another exercise with questions that are often found in tests of intelligence.

Instructions

Look carefully at the first three items of each sequence. Analyze how the second item changes from the first. How does the third change from the second? Make this same change to the third in order to find the fourth item you will write in the blank.

1.　　　AC　　　　CC　　　　EC　　　　＿＿＿

2.　　　2　　　　4　　　　8　　　　＿＿＿

3.　　　AFGA　　　CFGC　　　EFGE　　　＿＿＿

4.　　　6　　　　9　　　　13　　　　＿＿＿

5.　　　4　　　　9　　　　16　　　　＿＿＿

6.　　　24　　　　15　　　　8　　　　＿＿＿

7.

8.

9.

10.

15. VISUALLY ANALYZING GIVEN DATA

Good thinkers are good at drawing pictures in their minds. These pictures help them to summarize, clarify, and simplify large amounts of word or number information. In this exercise, the picture is given to you. Notice that its shape matches the given data. In other words, the shape, which in this case is a two-dimensional table, is perfect for displaying two variables. The names of people can be placed on one side of the table and their color choices can be placed on the other side.

Instructions

Use the tables and graphs provided with each question to determine your answer. For example, in question 1, use the following table to summarize the data about the colors that Tom, Dominick, Juanita, Fred, and Tina prefer. See if you can determine which color each person prefers.

1. Tom, Dominick, Juanita, Fred, and Tina each prefer a different color. The colors are red, yellow, blue, green, and orange. Juanita prefers yellow. Dominick doesn't like red or blue. Fred prefers green. Tina doesn't like blue.

Color	Person				
	Tom	Dominick	Juanita	Fred	Tina
Red			✗		
Blue			✗		
Yellow	✗	✗	✔	✗	✗
Orange			✗		
Green			✗		

Tom likes _____.   Fred likes _____.

Dominick likes _____.   Tina likes _____.

Juanita likes _____.

Instructions

In questions 2 and 3, the word data is given on a straight line, rather than on a table. On the straight lines below, write in a label at the end of each line (e.g., oldest-youngest, shortest-tallest). Now write in the names of the people in the correct position along the line to fit in with the given data.

2. Huang is older than Sam, but younger than Damian. Jack is younger than all three. Who is the second oldest?

```
┌──────────────┬──────────────┬──────────────┐
```

3. Jill was born 2 years after Tamika. Rita is 4 years older than Jill. Jean is 8 years younger than Rita. Tess was born a little after Jean. Who is the second oldest girl?

```
┌──────────┬──────────┬──────────┬──────────┐
```

4. Bill, Carlos, Mary, and Lan all love sports and games. One loves water sports, another is good at board games, one loves ball games, and the other loves gymnastics. Lan is great at chess and checkers, Mary loves water sports, and Bill doesn't like ball games. Find out which game or sport each person prefers.

Sport	Person			
	Bill	Carlos	Mary	Lan
Water Sports				
Board Games				
Ball Games				
Gymnastics				

5. Jasmine, Marcus, and Derek are professionals. One is an accountant, one is a computer programmer, and one is a music teacher. Marcus is not a computer programmer or an accountant. Derek is not an accountant. What are their jobs?

Job	Properties		
	Jasmine	Marcus	Derek
Accountant			
Programmer			
Music Teacher			

16. VISUALLY REPRESENTING PROPERTIES

In this exercise, some word information has been summarized for you with the help of a useful picture. The area in each circle represents a given property, such as black or animals. If something doesn't have this property, it lies outside the circle representing it.

1. If circle **B** (areas 1, 3, 4, 5) is the set of all things black, circle **T** (areas 2, 3, 4, 6) is the set of all things triangular, and circle **S** (areas 4, 5, 6, 7) is the set of all things small, then where would we find black triangles? In areas 3 and 4. Similarly, we would find small black things *other than triangles* in area 5.

In which numbered area(s) would we find

   a. small white triangles?
   b. large black triangles?
   c. small black circles?
   d. large white triangles?

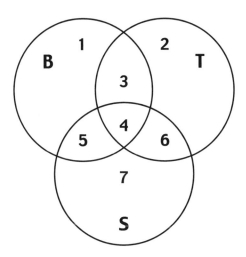

(continued)

2. In the second diagram, circle **A** represents animals, circle **L** represents things with legs, and circle **W** represents things with wings.

   In which numbered area(s) would we find

   a. ducks?
   b. horses?
   c. fish?
   d. snakes?
   e. ants?
   f. moths?

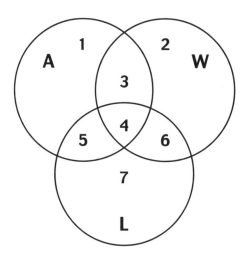

CHAPTER 4

EXERCISES TO IMPROVE CRITICAL THINKING

Critical thinking involves **asking yourself questions** about information in order to **make judgments** about it. For example, is the information fair, accurate, useful, truthful, or reliable? Remember the acronym **CAMPER** when you want to ask yourself some more probing questions when thinking critically. CAMPER comes from questioning or making judgments about the following items:

1. <u>C</u>onsequences: What are the <u>c</u>onsequences of this belief?

2. <u>A</u>ssumptions: What are the <u>a</u>ssumptions being made here?

3. <u>M</u>ain issue: What is the <u>m</u>ain issue being discussed here?

4. <u>P</u>rejudice: Is this information <u>p</u>rejudiced in any way?

5. <u>E</u>vidence and <u>e</u>xamples: What is the <u>e</u>vidence to support this viewpoint? What are <u>e</u>xamples of this?

6. <u>R</u>eliable and <u>r</u>elevant: How <u>r</u>eliable and <u>r</u>elevant is this evidence or information?

Good critical thinkers, like good creative thinkers, do more than ask themselves good questions. They have a good attitude or disposition when they ask themselves questions about an issue (Paul, 1992).

Good critical thinkers are **COOL**! That is, they try to

- <u>c</u>larify the issue and the meaning of things being considered.

- be <u>o</u>bjective about the issue by using facts, data, and examples.

- be <u>o</u>pen-minded or fair-minded by considering all viewpoints.

- be <u>l</u>oose by modifying their viewpoint if they hear new facts.

Critical thinking is very important in the world today. The world is so interdependent that we all have to be prepared to think **dialogically**. That is, we have to at least be prepared to consider the other person's or group's point of view. There are too many **monological** ("I am right—you are wrong") thinkers among children and adults.

Critical thinking runs through all of our intelligences (Gardner, 1993; Lazear, 1992). For example, visual thinkers make judgments about designs, and kinesthetic thinkers judge movements. Whatever our area of expertise, we should each strive to be a **COOL CAMPER!**

In exercises 17 through 25, you will learn some questions that you can use to **challenge** and judge the opinions of other people. And these same questions will help you to make **better judgments** about whether information is **fair**, **accurate**, **relevant**, **truthful**, and **reliable**—something you can be **sure of**.

17. DISTINGUISHING FACTS, NON–FACTS, AND OPINIONS

When you read a newspaper or magazine, do you believe that every statement is a fact? If you don't, how do you know which statements are facts and which ones are opinions? A non-fact is definitely not true, but an opinion may or may not be true. This exercise will help you identify some questions that critical thinkers use to identify facts from opinions.

It is a good idea to get other people to do this exercise and talk about how they know that a statement is fact or opinion. Ask them about the questions they unconsciously ask themselves when thinking about whether something is fact or opinion. Record their questions. Compare your list of questions with the ones given in Appendix A on page 149.

Instructions

Some statements in newspapers or magazines are facts (F), some are non-facts (NF), and some are opinions (O). The following list includes statements of all three kinds. Think about each statement and write F, NF, or O before each one.

___ 1. The sun is larger than the moon.

___ 2. Computers might become as small as molecules.

___ 3. The president of the United States should always be a man.

___ 4. The sun is more important to us than the moon.

___ 5. There will be a massive earthquake in China next year.

___ 6. Rocks are living things.

___ 7. There were more people in the world in 2000 than there were in 1999.

___ 8. Dogs make better pets than cats.

___ 9. All insects are harmful.

___ 10. Insects have six legs.

___ 11. We shouldn't produce electricity with nuclear reactors.

___ 12. We can produce electricity with nuclear reactors.

___ 13. The president of the United States has always been a man.

18. DISTINGUISHING AN UNSURE CONCLUSION FROM A DIRECT OBSERVATION

Many people make up their own conclusions when they see or read things even though they don't have any evidence to support them. It's easy to jump to conclusions when reading an advertisement or quickly glancing at a picture or story in the newspaper. Here are some examples to try. Don't jump to conclusions!

1. Write down three things that you CAN DEFINITELY BE SURE OF in the following cartoon. Does anyone disagree with you? What kinds of things can't you be sure of in pictures?

SURE OF . . .

a.＿＿＿＿＿＿＿＿＿＿

b.＿＿＿＿＿＿＿＿＿＿

c.＿＿＿＿＿＿＿＿＿＿

d.＿＿＿＿＿＿＿＿＿＿

CAN'T BE SURE OF . . .

a.＿＿＿＿＿＿＿＿＿＿

b.＿＿＿＿＿＿＿＿＿＿

c.＿＿＿＿＿＿＿＿＿＿

d.＿＿＿＿＿＿＿＿＿＿

2. What can you DEFINITELY BE SURE OF in the following written advertisement? Underline these words.

   Now look at the ad and circle the words that you CAN'T BE SURE OF because they could be interpreted in different ways.

Everything will be sold at City Mart for half price on Friday.

3. A man saw a boy run quickly out of a shop and knock a girl down. The boy did not stop to help. Which two of the following can you be SURE OF? Circle the two letters.

   a. The girl was about to go inside the shop.
   b. The boy is late for some reason.
   c. The boy had been in the shop.
   d. The man saw the girl get knocked down.

4. For each of the following events write down three conclusions that people might make to explain them. Choose any one as your conclusion, and write down on a separate sheet of paper what evidence is needed to prove that it is the correct conclusion.

   a. Your flashlight doesn't work when you switch it on.

   Possible conclusions:

   _____

   _____

   _____

b. The hardware store is having a "going out of business" sale.

Possible conclusions:

_____

_____

_____

c. The number of nuclear power stations in the world increases each year.

Possible conclusions:

_____

_____

_____

d. In some countries it is against the law to use freon gas in aerosol spray cans.

Possible conclusions:

_____

_____

_____

e. In a supermarket you can buy a carton of brand A margarine for $1.20. The same amount of brand B margarine is only $1.00.

Possible conclusions:

_____

_____

_____

f. Pandas are almost extinct.

Possible conclusions:

_____

_____

_____

19. CHALLENGING THE RELIABILITY OF A CLAIM

We sometimes read in newspaper or magazine reports that someone claims to have seen an unidentified flying object or a strange creature, such as Bigfoot or the Loch Ness monster. Your first thought is to ask yourself, "How reliable is this newspaper?" or "How reliable is the person who wrote this article?"

Naturally, we want some proof or evidence before we believe such reports. A good critical thinker would have some really useful questions to ask the person making the claim. Here is your chance to think about your questions for judging the reliability of a claim. Other people might have more questions that you can add to your list.

Instructions

1. There is a story in the newspaper about a man who claims he saw an animal that looked like a dinosaur in the stream in a remote part of his farm. Write down at least five questions you would like him to answer before you believe his claim. Check with other people, and make a large list of probing questions that could be useful for challenging the reliability of a claim.

2. In the following paragraph, underline any evidence that helps you BELIEVE the claim. Circle any evidence here that causes you to DOUBT that the claim is true.

Claim: In 1960, Tor MacLeod claimed that he saw the Loch Ness monster through his binoculars. The large gray mass was about 1 mile away on the opposite shore of Loch Ness, which is a very deep lake in Scotland. The monster had three elephant-like trunks at the front. MacLeod was not accompanied by any of his friends. He had moved to the area to live because he wanted to view the monster before he died. He viewed the monster for about 8 minutes. The weather was dull and overcast with drizzling rain. He wore a new overcoat and hat to keep himself warm. MacLeod phoned the newspaper immediately after seeing the monster. The newspaper had just been taken over by a new owner.

3. In the following paragraph, underline any evidence that helps you to BELIEVE the claim. Circle any evidence that causes you to DOUBT the claim.

   Claim: On November 2, 1957, in Levelland, Texas, a family reported seeing a flying saucer. They said it appeared on the ground near their car at about 10 o'clock at night. The car was a new one and in very good condition. The family members were on their way home after watching an air show during the day. They watched the saucer for about 5 minutes. Several hours later, another person saw the saucer in a nearby town. The family said that the engine of their car stopped as the saucer came near. An electrical thunderstorm was in the area at the time of their sighting. The father called the editor of the local newspaper. During the week before the family's sighting, the paper had run a series of articles on flying saucers.

20. DISTINGUISHING RELEVANT FROM IRRELEVANT INFORMATION

Something is **relevant** if it helps you to achieve a goal or some purpose you have in mind. For example, what are some relevant factors to consider in choosing a new bike? Choosing a bike is your goal. Is the price relevant? Yes. How about the time of day you buy it? No. The more relevant factors or things you can come up with, the better your decision will be. First, you have to be clear about your goal. Next, you have to identify what is really important and why.

Instructions

1. Imagine you have lost your dog. Circle the letters in front of the three MOST IMPORTANT, or RELEVANT, things about your dog that you think would help people find it.

   a. Where you got the dog.
   b. The breed of the dog.
   c. What the dog eats.
   d. Where the dog sleeps at night.
   e. The color of the dog.
   f. The sex of the dog.
   g. The height of the dog.
   h. How fast the dog can run.

2. You want to apply for an after-school job delivering newspapers. The manager asks you to write down some relevant things about yourself that will help you to be considered for the job. Circle the letters in front of three things that you think would be MOST IMPORTANT to mention in this situation.

   a. You are left-handed.
   b. You are good at science.
   c. You are a healthy person.
   d. You are 12 years old.
   e. You are a member of the school basketball team.
   f. You live in the neighborhood.
   g. You have a new bicycle.

3. You want to buy a breakfast cereal that is good for your health. Circle the letters in front of three things you think are MOST RELEVANT to consider when making your choice.

   a. The box is made from recycled paper.
   b. Famous people eat this cereal.
   c. It contains high fiber.
   d. The company is a sponsor of the Olympic Games.
   e. It tastes good.

    f. It doesn't have any preservatives.

    g. It comes in serving-sized packets.

4. Imagine you have the job of spending a large sum of money to buy some land for a farm. What are five VERY IMPORTANT or RELEVANT characteristics of the land that you would consider before buying it?

  a._____   d._____

  b._____   e._____

  c._____

5. You have to design a new toy for 3- to 5-year-old children. What are five VERY IMPORTANT or RELEVANT features that such a toy should have? Give a reason for each choice.

FEATURE   **REASON**

  a._____   _____

  b._____   _____

  c._____   _____

  d._____   _____

  e._____   _____

21. THINKING CRITICALLY ABOUT WHAT YOU READ

Good critical thinkers think about the **consequences** of doing something, the **assumptions** being made, the **main** point of an issue, any **prejudice** or bias in picture or word information, the **evidence** and **examples** available, the **relevance** of factors and statements, and the **reliability** of the sources of information. The first letters of these things, we recall, spell out **CAMPER**. Remember this acronym, and what it stands for, when judging an article or when debating an issue with others. Challenge them by saying, "Give me an example of . . ." or "Where is your evidence for that statement?" Try challenging the author of the following letter to the editor, which addresses a well-known issue.

Instructions

A farmer wrote this letter to the editor of a newspaper. It is meant to stir the emotions of some people. UNDERLINE the words you would challenge in this letter as being too emotional or opinionated. Assume that you agree with daylight savings time and have to debate or argue with this farmer about it. What are some QUESTIONS you would ask him in order to highlight the weaknesses in his letter?

When daylight savings time came to an end once more a few weeks ago, we could almost hear the sigh of relief from the vast majority of citizens. Yes, I know that 16 years ago a sizable majority voted in favor of introducing this ridiculous interference with our timekeeping. Now we have learned from bitter experience how many problems it has created.

I acknowledge that there are still a handful who would like to continue with this outdated dinosaur. But what about other citizens? This is supposed to be a democracy, which means that the wishes of the majority should be paramount. I am sure that dairy farmers don't like it, and mothers with young babies hate it.

Questions to ask:

_____

_____

_____

_____

_____

22. MAKING A DECISION

Decision making is about using relevant criteria to make a choice between different possibilities. The process involves six steps:

1. Clearly identify what you have to make a decision about.

2. Identify the choices or alternatives.

3. List the good and bad things about each choice.

4. Find relevant criteria for comparing the choices.

5. Rate each choice according to the criteria.

6. Make a decision by selecting the best possible choice (i.e., the choice with the most rating points).

The following exercise will help you use these steps.

Instructions

Step 1. WHAT do we have to make a decision about in each of the following situations?

a. Some aerosol spray cans contain a gas called Freon that destroys the earth's ozone layer, which protects us from harmful cancer-causing rays from the sun.

   We have to decide _____.

b. The world's oil supply for making gasoline for cars is rapidly being depleted.

   We have to decide _____.

Step 2. List three or more ALTERNATIVES we can choose from when deciding how to solve each of the following problems.

a. It is becoming very difficult to dispose of all the garbage that people make in their homes each week.

We can _____, _____,
or _____.

b. More and more homes are being broken into in our suburbs.

We can _____, _____,
or _____.

Step 3. Sources for producing electricity include oil, steam, solar, or nuclear energy. List one ADVANTAGE and one DISADVANTAGE for each of these sources.

ENERGY SOURCE	ADVANTAGE	DISADVANTAGE
a. oil		
b. steam		
c. solar power		
d. nuclear energy		

Steps 4, 5, and 6. You have won a vacation to one of four countries. You run quickly through the first three steps of the decision-making process.

(Step 1) Which country will I choose?
(Step 2) I may choose India, Australia, Italy, or Fiji.
(Step 3) I will list one ADVANTAGE and one DISADVANTAGE about going to each country.

COUNTRY	ADVANTAGE	DISADVANTAGE
a. India		
b. Australia		
c. Italy		
d. Fiji		

Step 4. From the list of advantages and disadvantages about the countries, write down four RELEVANT CRITERIA that you would consider in comparing and rating the four countries.

My relevant criteria for comparing are:

a._____   c._____
b._____   d._____

Step 5. Write your four criteria in the table below. Now rate each country on how it meets each criterion, using a scale of 1–4 points (1 = doesn't meet criterion; 4 = completely meets criterion). When you have rated each country, write the total rating points for each country in the last row of the table.

Your Criteria	India	Australia	Italy	Fiji
1.				
2.				
3.				
4.				
Total Rating Points				

Step 6. My decision is to go to _____ because it has the highest overall rating points.

23. IDENTIFYING CAUSES AND EFFECTS

Critical thinkers try to clarify information. Many people can't even recognize an effect, or a result, and the causes that bring it about. Can you?

1. In the story below, one of the events CAUSED one of the other events to happen. Underline the letter in front of the CAUSE and circle the letter in front of its EFFECT.

   a. A boy went fishing at the lake.
   b. He went with a friend.
   c. He ate some green berries.
   d. He didn't catch any fish.
   e. He was late coming home.
   f. The next day he was very sick.

2. Underline the CAUSE and circle the EFFECT in the following sentences.

   a. The brontosaurus ran into the lake as the tyrannosaurus came over the hill.

   b. The brontosaurus, with its large body and small head, ate for most of the day before leaving the lake.

3. Write in the missing CAUSE or EFFECT in the following table.

CAUSE	EFFECT
_____ _____	causes fruit to ripen on trees.
When sap stops flowing in trees,	_____ _____
Nectar is on the flowers of plants to	_____ _____

24. CONSIDERING OTHER POINTS OF VIEW

In an argument, some people see only their own point of view. They don't want to hear the other person say why he or she believes something else. The critical thinker is more tolerant and is prepared to at least listen to other points of view. Fights and even wars start because people don't want to listen to other points of view. If they did, they might hear some new facts, and they might understand the feelings of other people.

1. Some people think that farmers should not spray insecticides on their crops. Many farmers think that they should. Write two reasons why farmers SHOULDN'T and two reasons why farmers SHOULD spray insecticides on their crops.

   Why they shouldn't:
   a. _____
   b. _____

Why they should:

a. _____

b. _____

2. Some people think that it is wrong for some countries to allow whales to be killed. The people who hunt the whales believe they should be allowed to kill them. Write two reasons why people SHOULDN'T kill whales and two reasons why people from some countries SHOULD be able to kill whales.

Why they shouldn't kill whales:

a. _____

b. _____

Why they should be able to kill whales:

a. _____

b. _____

25. ASKING YOUR OWN QUESTIONS

Most students wait to answer questions rather than asking their own. And yet, the more questions you can ask yourself about something you read or hear, the greater your understanding of the topic.

When you ask questions, you pay careful attention and make connections with things you already know. The better your questions, the better your thinking—especially your critical thinking.

Instructions

1. Close your eyes and put your finger on a word in row 1. Open your eyes and memorize it. Close your eyes and put your finger on a word in row 2. Open your eyes and memorize it.

Now make up a question about EARTHQUAKES starting with the two words, or question starters, you have put your finger on. Can you look up an answer for your question?

Row 1:

Who   Why   How   Where   Which   What

Row 2:

Would   Can   Will   Is   Did   Might

Example:

Q: HOW WOULD scientists measure the severity of an earthquake?

A: They use an instrument called a seismograph that measures the amount of movement during an earthquake.

Now write down your question about earthquakes (if you aren't familiar with earthquakes, try another topic). Try to answer your question.

Q:_____

A:_____

Here is another method for making up your own questions about a topic. In this case, the topic is WHALES.

2. Write five words (in the five blank boxes on page 62) that you think of when you hear the word WHALES.

   Now write one to five words above or below these boxes. These words will connect your words to the topic of WHALES. The words should make a sensible sentence, starting with WHALES and ending with the word in the box.

   In the example, the topic is "whales," the related word is "migrate," and the connector is "swim large distances to." The statement is "Whales swim large distances to migrate."

   Now ask either "Why?" or "How?" of each sentence you make and write your questions. For example: "Why do whales swim large distances to migrate?"

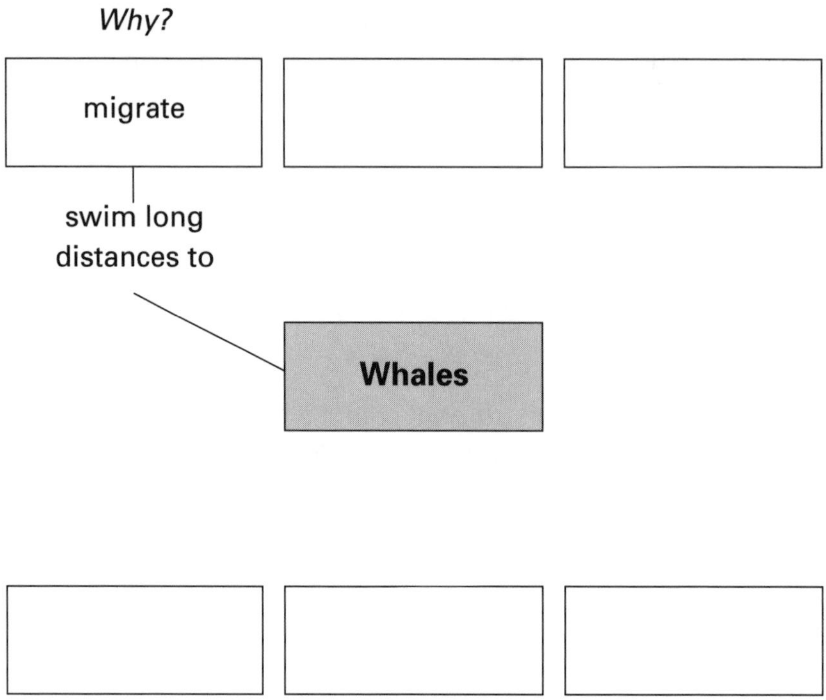

Why?

migrate		

swim long
distances to

Whales

Questions about whales:

Q1. _____

Q2. _____

Q3. _____

Q4. _____

Q5. _____

3. Repeat question 2 for the topic of IRON. Try to find answers to your own questions.

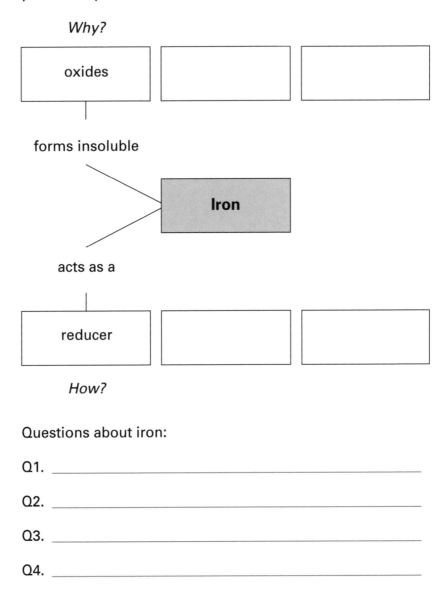

Why?

oxides

forms insoluble

Iron

acts as a

reducer

How?

Questions about iron:

Q1. _____

Q2. _____

Q3. _____

Q4. _____

Instructions

All you are given in this question is the information that Jack earns $800 a month and his savings are $400 a month. Normally, a teacher would ask questions that required you to analyze and use this information. Imagine that you are the teacher and create two questions using this information. Write your questions below, along with a description of the math processes (+, −, x or ÷) needed to solve each problem. How many more questions can you create for this information?

4. Write down two questions using these data. Say which math processes (+, −, x, or ÷) are needed to answer your questions.

   Jack EARNS $800 a month. His EXPENSES are $400 a month.

   Q1. _____

   Math processes needed:

   _____

   _____

   Q2. _____

   Math processes needed:

   _____

   _____

CHAPTER 5

EXERCISES TO IMPROVE
CREATIVE THINKING

Why is creative thinking so hard to do? Would you believe that it is your brain that sometimes makes creative thinking difficult?

In exercises 1 through 12, you saw how good the human brain is at **organizing** and **storing** the **usual properties** of something. Think of a chair. Your brain immediately **recalls** something with four legs, a flat seat, and a back support. These are the usual properties. Now, if you are given the task of building a creative chair, your brain stops you from making a chair with one leg and no back support! This isn't the usual picture you have in your mind.

Your brain can make it hard for you to escape from the picture or pattern you have in your mind. **Creative thinking** involves **breaking away** from usual patterns stored in your memory. Think of the acronym **CREATE** when you want to think creatively! This acronym will remind you of the six kinds of creative thinking you can do when you need to try a little creative problem solving.

<u>C</u>ombine: Can I <u>c</u>ombine some things in a new way?
<u>R</u>everse: Can I <u>r</u>everse some parts or processes here?
<u>E</u>liminate: Can I <u>e</u>liminate or remove some part or process?
<u>A</u>lternative: Can I use <u>a</u>lternative methods or materials?
<u>T</u>wist: Can I <u>t</u>wist things around a bit?
<u>E</u>laborate: Can I <u>e</u>laborate or add something?

These are some good questions that creative people often ask themselves when they want to break away. Exercise 26 encourages you to fantasize by suggesting possible future consequences. Exercise 27 will help you try some reverse thinking to break those usual patterns. This really frustrates your brain. Exercise 28 offers some problems that might be solved with our acronym **CREATE**. If you can solve question 3 in exercise 28—the one about joining the nine dots with four straight lines—you have really escaped the patterns in your brain. By the way, creative thinkers are also **FIRST**! They have the following characteristics:

Fantasize: They fantasize or try unreal ideas.

Incubate: They often incubate or think about an idea for a long time.

Risks: They take risks, despite what other people think.

Sensitive: They are sensitive to the creativity of nature and humans.

Trigger: They try to trigger new ways of thinking about things by being playful and having fun with ideas.

And finally, exercise 29 encourages you to be more **sensitive** to the creativity of nature and human beings. This exercise poses the same questions that passed through the minds of the first people to make a pencil, a newspaper, a stoplight, and a coffee mug. Everything around us has a form that fits a particular function (Perkins, 1986). In other words, a pencil has six sides, a tree has thousands of leaves, *for a reason*—not just by chance. If you think about it, you see that these design features fit particular functions.

Remember to observe the size, color, use, materials, parts, and shape (**SCUMPS** is the acronym to remember) of the things around you. Then you should ask yourself **why** these things have these properties instead of alternative properties. You will start to be sensitive to the creativity in the world around you.

The properties, or **attributes**, summarized by the acronym SCUMPS often give you some ideas for the **creative uses** of objects. This thinking process is called **attribute listing**. For example, a brick is rough, so it could be used as a pencil sharpener; is geometric, suggesting use as a wedge, support, seat, or stencil; is heavy, suggesting use as a door stop, paperweight, or anchor; has holes, so it could be used as a pencil holder; and is hard, suggesting use as a hammer or weapon.

When is the best time to do some creative thinking? Well, your brain must be relaxed for creative thinking. Some good times for creative thinking are when you are just waking up or dozing off or when you are taking a morning shower. Focus on a problem at these moments and you'll be more likely to come up with creative solutions. At these times, you have the right endorphins, or brain chemicals, and also the theta brain waves that appear to be needed for breaking away.

26. CREATIVE CONSEQUENCES

Let's see if you can fantasize. This "if . . . then" exercise will give you a chance to dream a little. Notice that other people will dream up different consequences than you do. As in all tests of creativity, there is no one correct answer here.

Instructions

1. Complete the following by placing words in the blanks.

a. If there were no more birds in the world, then _____

_____.

And this would mean that _____

_____.

b. If the earth no longer had a moon, then _____

_____.

And this would mean that _____

_____.

c. If there were no longer any oil deposits on earth, then _____

_____.

And this would mean that _____

_____.

d. If there were no longer any whales on earth, then _____

_____.

And this would mean that _____

_____.

27. REVERSE CREATIVE THINKING

Creative thinkers often try an idea that is just the opposite of what most people would try. They try **reverse thinking**. This really loosens up the fixed patterns you have stored in your brain. Your brain remembers what you can photograph or what you can see, but it struggles when it has to come up with things you can't photograph or can't see.

Instructions

1. List three things that you COULD NOT photograph with your camera.

    a. _____
    b. _____
    c. _____

2. List three ways of opening a book WITHOUT holding it with your hands?

    a. _____
    b. _____
    c. _____

3. What are three reasons why a person might be seen reading a newspaper turned UPSIDE DOWN?

   a. _____
   b. _____
   c. _____

4. What are three ways in which a car and a tree are the SAME?

   a. _____
   b. _____
   c. _____

5. List three things that you WOULD NOT find in America.

   a. _____
   b. _____
   c. _____

28. CREATIVE PROBLEM SOLVING

Creative problem solving demands that you find answers that are not normal or predictable. You have to CREATE. You might even be the first person to come up with an idea.

Instructions

1. Can you think of three or more good ideas for changing the design and packaging of a box of breakfast cereal in order to make it more interesting to people? Think of what the letters in CREATE stand for.

   a. _____
   b. _____
   c. _____

2. Can you think of three ways of getting a Ping-Pong ball from the bottom of a 3-foot-long vertical pipe whose end is stuck in concrete? The pipe is only slightly wider than the ball. You cannot destroy the pipe, the ball, or the concrete.

a. _____

b. _____

c. _____

3. Put your pencil on dot A. Now, without taking your pencil from the paper, join these nine dots using no more than 4 straight lines, continuously connected.

```
        •       •       •



        •       •       •



  A     •       •       •
```

29. ANALYZING THE CREATIVITY OF DESIGNS

Creative people are sensitive to the creativity about them. That is, they notice the design of things created by humans or by nature. Everything around us has a design that fits a particular function. The more you carefully observe things and ask yourself why they have a particular shape, color, size, material, or part, the more sensitive to creativity you will be.

1. Why do pencils usually have 6 sides rather than 3 or 10?

2. Why does a tree have thousands of leaves rather than four or five?

3. Why are newspaper pages so big compared with the pages of a book?

4. Why are drinking cups made of clay rather than steel?

5. Why do dogs and cats have four legs rather than two?

6. Why is the color red used to indicate danger?

SECTION II

APPLYING THINKING PROCESSES
TO NEW CONTENT

By now, you have learned a number of good questions to ask yourself when you want to think about a certain topic or thing. You need these "**thinking questions**" if you want to be better at thinking.

This section of the book mixes up all the different ways of thinking you have tried in exercises 1 through 29. You will use these thinking processes in considering various interesting topics. The type of thinking involved with each question is written in **BOLDFACE CAPITALS**. You may be unable to answer a question because you might not understand the content or possess information about the topic. In that case, you will have to ask a teacher or parent for assistance. On the other hand, you may be unable to answer a question because you don't know the right questions to ask yourself. If this is the case, go back to the exercise in the first section of the book that describes the thinking process you are struggling with. Read through the beginning exercise and then try the question again.

Good luck! The following questions are not easy. They make you think rather than just remember facts. Some of the questions have more than one answer. Remember, you can learn to think better and more intelligently. Be confident. You have a brain that can be as powerful as a **supercomputer** when you provide it with good thinking questions.

CHAPTER 6

ANIMALS

Living things are either plants or animals. Therefore, fish, birds, insects, reptiles, and mammals are all animals. About one million different animals have been identified—from one-celled microscopic creatures to large mammals that weigh thousands of pounds. Most animals move around the earth and feed on plants or other animals. Most plants, on the other hand, are fixed to the ground by roots and make their own food from water, carbon dioxide, and sunlight.

Animals can be cold- or warm-blooded, live on or in water or land, be helpful or harmful to humans, and contain a variety of body parts to help them to survive. A mammal is an animal that has a backbone, is warm-blooded, and feeds its young with the milk of the mother. The most intelligent mammal is the human. Apart from birds and mammals, most animals are cold-blooded.

For years, humans have killed animals for food and for other reasons. Today, however, many rare or endangered animals are being protected in an effort to keep them from becoming extinct.

1. CATEGORIZING

The animals listed here belong to two groups. Circle the three names that belong in one of the groups and explain why that group differs from the other.

rabbit   lion   cow   horse   shark   dog

Different because:

_____

_____

2. ORDERING

The following animals have been placed in an ORDER. What PROPERTY was used in determining this order?

worms   rats   whales   humans

Property used:

_____

_____

3. IDENTIFYING ASSUMPTIONS

A girl found a dead bird in her driveway. She concluded that it must have been killed by a cat.

What is she assuming? (What else may have killed the bird?) What evidence would she need to help prove her conclusion?

_____

_____

_____

_____

4. ANALYZING DESIGNS

Why do you think a cat has four legs rather than two?

_____

_____

5. GENERALIZING AND LOOKING FOR PATTERNS

Snakes, birds, frogs, humans, and fish are all animals. List as many parts of these different animals as possible. Now cross out the ones that are NOT COMMON TO ALL of these animals. What generalization can you make about animals?

Parts:

_____

_____

Generalization: All animals

_____

_____

6. ANALYZING PARTS AND RELATIONSHIPS

Complete the following so that the last two things are related in the same way as the first two things.

Rose is to flower as eagle is to _____.

Sparrow is to fly as shark is to _____.

Snake is to hiss as dog is to _____.

7. CREATIVE CONSEQUENCES

Complete the following sentences by placing words in the blanks.

If there were no more birds in the world, then_____

_____.

And this would mean that _____

_____.

8. CONSIDERING OTHER POINTS OF VIEW

Write down a reason FOR and a reason AGAINST allowing hunters to kill elephants.

For:

_____

_____

Against:

_____

_____

9. CREATIVE REVERSALS

Can you think of three things that cats can NEVER do?

a. _____

b. _____

c. _____

10. COMPARING

Write three ways in which a crab is the SAME as a fish. Both:

a. _____

b. _____

c. _____

Now write three ways in which it is DIFFERENT from a fish. Only crabs:

a. _____

b. _____

c. _____

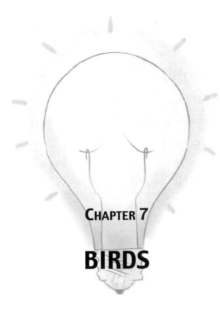

CHAPTER 7

BIRDS

Birds are feathered animals. Although all birds have wings, some of the heavier birds are unable to fly. Birds help farmers by eating insects, but they can also be unhelpful by eating crops such as fruits. All birds hatch from eggs that are kept in a nest. Most birds lay about 10 or 20 eggs a year (although one domesticated bird, the chicken, can lay up to 250 eggs a year).

Because birds are warm-blooded like human beings, they often wash themselves in pools of water to keep cool in the summer months. In winter, some kinds of birds migrate, or fly thousands of miles, to find food and to have their young in warmer climates. Birds use calls to tell each other where they are, to warn of danger, and to communicate other information.

1. IDENTIFYING KEY WORDS

Write down five words that have something to do with BIRDS. Add some words suggested by other people.

a. nest   d._____

b. _____   e._____

c. _____   f._____

2. MAKING CONNECTIONS

Write a key word from question 1 at the end of each row on the following table. Then write two to six words as a connector to make a sensible sentence.

TOPIC	CONNECTOR	KEY WORD
Birds	lay eggs in a	nest
Birds	_____	_____
Birds	_____	_____

3. ASKING YOUR OWN QUESTIONS

Now ask WHY or HOW of each sentence you made in question 2. Write down your questions and try to answer them.

Q: WHY do birds lay eggs in a nest?
A: To keep them warm and away from enemies.

Q: _____
A: _____

Q: _____
A: _____

4. ORDERING

The following things have been placed in an ORDER. What PROPERTY was used in determining this order?

leaves   caterpillar   bird   cat

Property used:

_____

_____

5. JUDGING RELEVANCE

A boy has lost his bird. He writes a "lost bird" notice to place in shop windows near his home. Underline only the parts of the following notice that you think are useful or relevant in helping find the pet bird.

"My bird is named Tommy. I bought him last year. He cost me $10.00. He has black feathers and a yellow beak. He is a parrot. Tommy lives in a cage with three other birds. At night he whistles after he is fed."

6. MAKING A DECISION

Imagine you have to choose a classroom pet—either a mouse, a bird, or a goldfish. List an ADVANTAGE and a DISADVANTAGE for each of these classroom pets.

PET	ADVANTAGE	DISADVANTAGE
mouse		
bird		
goldfish		

From these advantages and disadvantages, select three or more IMPORTANT THINGS, or factors, that a class should consider in selecting a classroom pet.

a. _____   c. _____

b. _____

Now consider each of these factors. Give three points to the pet that you think is best suited for each factor, two points to the second best suited, and one point to the worst pet for each factor. Which pet has the most points?

Factor	Animal		
	Mouse	Bird	Goldfish
1			
2			
3			
Total Points			

7. CATEGORIZING

One of the birds in each group is DIFFERENT from the others. Circle the different bird and say WHY it is different.

GROUP	REASON FOR DIFFERENCE
a. eagle, sparrow, pigeon	_____
b. ostrich, magpie, penguin	_____
c. duck, pelican, hawk	_____

8. CREATIVE ALTERNATIVES

List two or more ways of keeping a bird outside without putting it in a cage.

a. _____

b. _____

9. GENERALIZING

In the table below, write "yes" for each of the properties that each of the listed birds has. What generalization can you make about birds?

Birds	Properties					
	Has a Nest	Has Two Legs	Has a Beak	Can Fly	Lays Eggs	Eats Meat
Ostrich						
Parakeet						
Sparrow						
Eagle						
Pigeon						

Generalization: All birds:

_____

_____

10. CONSIDERING OTHER POINTS OF VIEW

Lucia wants a parrot as a pet. Her mother does not want a bird as a pet. Write two reasons FOR and two reasons AGAINST Lucia's buying a pet parrot.

Reasons for:

a. _____

b. _____

Reasons against:

a. _____

b. _____

11. PREDICTING

What type of food does a bird eat and where do you think it finds the food if . . .

a. it has a short, strong beak and can fly?

_____

b. it has webbed feet and a long beak?

_____

c. it has small claws and a long, thin, curved beak?

_____

d. it has long, curved claws and a curved, sharp beak?

_____

CHAPTER 8

COMMUNICATIONS

Communication is the sharing of information. We can communicate by speaking, writing, signalling, drawing, using our faces and bodies, and so on. Cave paintings were one of the first methods of communication for recording, as well as sharing, information. Through the use of satellites, cables, optical fibers, and other electronic inventions, we can now instantly communicate around the world to billions of people at the same time. E-mail, faxes, and the Internet are very recent inventions that have changed how we communicate with each other.

We have come a long way from the drawings that cave dwellers used to communicate with each other. The hieroglyphics of the ancient Egyptians were a large step forward in visually recording information. The printing press invented in the 1400s was another giant leap forward because it provided a way to produce books mechanically. Before the press was invented, the few books that were produced were created by hand. Books were usually owned only by the wealthy, and relatively few people knew how to read. In more modern times, newspapers and public libraries are just two ways printed communication is made available to everyone.

1. COMPARING

Write three ways in which a newspaper is the SAME as a book. Both:

a. _____

b. _____

c. _____

Now write three ways in which it is DIFFERENT from a book. Only newspapers:

a. _____

b. _____

c. _____

2. ORDERING

The following things have been placed in an ORDER. What PROPERTY was used in determining this order?

letter   newspaper   book   encyclopedia

Property used:

_____

_____

3. DISTINGUISHING FACTS FROM OPINIONS

One of the following sentences is a FACT. Underline this fact.

a. Television is more interesting than radio.

b. Radio was invented before television.

c. You can learn better from a book than you can from TV.

d. Eventually, there will be no need for newspapers.

Why is it a fact?

_____

_____

4. IDENTIFYING ASSUMPTIONS

Mr. Lee wondered why his newspaper was not in his driveway in the morning. He assumed that the paper delivery person was sick.

a. What is Mr. Lee's assumption about what happened to the delivery person?

_____

_____

b. Why do you think Mr. Lee chose this reason?

_____

_____

c. What evidence would you need to prove that Mr. Lee is correct?

_____

_____

5. GENERALIZING AND LOOKING FOR PATTERNS

Make a big list of PROPERTIES that all of these types of media have in common. Then cross out any properties NOT COMMON to all of the items.

RADIO	NEWSPAPER	BOOK	TELEVISION
_____	_____	_____	_____
_____	_____	_____	_____
_____	_____	_____	_____
_____	_____	_____	_____
_____	_____	_____	_____

Are there any properties that all of these items have in common?

Generalization: All media:

_____

_____

6. ANALYZING DESIGNS

Why do you think many road signs use black writing on a yellow background?

_____

_____

7. CREATIVE CONSEQUENCES

Complete the following sentences by placing words in the blanks.

If there were no more computers in the world, then _____

_____.

And this would mean that _____

_____.

8. CONSIDERING OTHER POINTS OF VIEW

Write down a reason FOR and a reason AGAINST using the Internet.

a. Reason for:

_____

_____

b. Reason against:

_____

_____

Share your reasons. Can you defend the reason you gave for not wanting to use the Internet?

_____

_____

9. CREATIVE REVERSALS

Can you think of three places where you COULDN'T read a newspaper?

a. _____

b. _____

c. _____

10. IDENTIFYING KEY WORDS

Write five words that have something to do with TELEVISION. Add some words suggested by other people.

a. advertising   d. _____

b._____   e. _____

c._____   f. _____

11. MAKING CONNECTIONS

Write a key word from question 10 at the end of each row on the following table. Then write two to six words as a connector to make a sensible sentence.

TOPIC	CONNECTOR	KEY WORD
Television	is used for	advertising.
Television	_____	_____
Television	_____	_____

12. ASKING YOUR OWN QUESTIONS

Now ask WHY or HOW of each sentence you made in question 11. Write down your questions and try to answer them.

Q: WHY is television used for advertising?
A: Because many people watch TV and can see products in color, with movement, and with sound.

Q: _____
A: _____

Q: _____
A: _____

CHAPTER 9

DINOSAURS

Dinosaurs were cold-blooded reptiles that lived on Earth 65 to 220 million years ago, when the Earth was generally warm and humid. Some ate plants, while others ate meat. Some were 90 feet long and would have been able to look over a three-story building, while others were less than 3 feet long. Some weighed 80 tons—10 times the weight of an African elephant.

The bones and footprints of dinosaurs were covered with mud millions of years ago. Under the pressure of layers, these dinosaur remains turned into hard rock. Today scientists find very old bones, footprints, and shells in this rock that help them picture what life was like millions of years ago. These preserved bones and prints are called fossils.

Some dinosaurs, such as tyrannosaurus, did not like the water, while others, such as brontosaurus, spent time in lakes. Here are some more properties of five kinds of dinosaurs:

Dinosaurs	Properties					
	Sharp Teeth	Neck Length	Number of Legs	Small Brain	Laid Eggs	Ate Meat
Tyrannosaurus	yes	short	4	yes	yes	yes
Brontosaurus	no	long	4	yes	yes	no
Stegosaurus	no	short	4	yes	yes	no
Anatosaurus	no	short	4	yes	yes	no
Triceratops	no	short	4	yes	yes	no

1. COMPARING

Write three ways in which a dinosaur is the SAME as an elephant. Both:

a. _____

b. _____

c. _____

Now write three ways in which it is DIFFERENT. Only dinosaurs:

a. _____

b. _____

c. _____

2. DISTINGUISHING FACTS FROM OPINIONS

Underline the two sentences that are FACTS and say WHY they are facts.

a. Dinosaurs were not warm-blooded.

b. Dinosaurs became extinct because smaller animals ate their eggs.

c. Someday scientists will breed dinosaurs in the laboratory.

d. Dinosaurs needed oxygen to live.

Why are they facts?

_____

_____

3. IDENTIFYING ASSUMPTIONS

Mary concluded that dinosaurs became extinct because smaller animals learned to find dinosaur eggs and then ate them. What was Mary assuming? What else could have caused dinosaurs to become extinct?

_____

_____

4. GENERALIZING AND LOOKING FOR PATTERNS

Allosaurus was a dinosaur. Using your own knowledge and the table of facts about dinosaurs on page 91, list four things you can be SURE OF about allosaurus.

a. _____

b. _____

c. _____

d. _____

Megasaurus is a reptile in South America that lays eggs, has four legs, eats plants, and has a small brain. Is it a dinosaur? Why or why not?

_____

_____

5. ANALYZING DESIGNS

a. Why did the brontosaurus need such a long neck?

_____

_____

b. Why did dinosaurs, like other reptiles, lay eggs rather than have live babies?

_____

_____

6. REVERSE THINKING

Name two types of animals that tyrannosaurus COULD NOT catch and eat easily.

a. _____

b. _____

The ANSWER is dinosaur. Make up two questions with this answer.

Q: _____

Q: _____

7. IDENTIFYING CAUSES AND EFFECTS

Separate the CAUSES from EFFECTS by circling the effect in each of the following:

a. The brontosaurus, with its large body and small head, ate during most of the day.

b. The brontosaurus went into the lake as the tyrannosaurus came over the hill.

8. PREDICTING

a. Using the table of facts about dinosaurs on page 91, predict which type of dinosaur was the LAST to become extinct on earth. State your reason why.

Last to become extinct:

_____

Reason:

_____

_____

b. The dinosaur camptosaurus protected itself by running and hiding behind trees. What do you predict about its . . .

1. size?

_____

_____

2. food?

_____

_____

3. teeth?

_____

_____

c. The dinosaur stegosaurus had soft teeth, couldn't run quickly, couldn't swim, and couldn't hide easily. How do you think it protected itself?

_____

_____

d. If a dinosaur had sharp teeth and webbed feet, what do you think it ate? Why?

_____

_____

(continued)

9. CREATIVE CONSEQUENCES

Complete the following sentences by placing words in the blanks:

If there were dinosaurs in the world today, then _____

_____.

And this would mean that_____

_____.

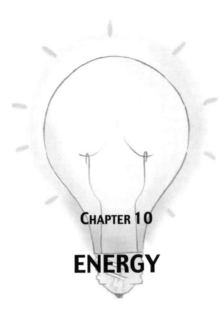

CHAPTER 10

ENERGY

Something has energy if it has the capacity to do work. The sun is a major supplier of energy to animals and plants on Earth. Humans also get energy from chemicals, electricity, machines, tides, wind, and nuclear reactions. Primitive people used fire, wind, and animals as sources of energy to help them do work. As the earth's deposits of oil, gas, and coal are used up, humans will have to use more solar and nuclear energy for making electricity to power electrical machines.

1. COMPARING

Write three ways in which sound energy is the SAME as light energy. Now write three ways in which sound energy is DIFFERENT from light energy.

Both Sound and Light:	Only Sound:
a._____	a._____
b._____	b._____
c._____	c._____

2. ORDERING

Place the following things in an ORDER. Indicate which PROPERTY you used in determining this order.

light   heat   sound

Your order:

_____

Property used:

_____

3. JUDGING RELEVANCE

Write down one ADVANTAGE and one DISADVANTAGE for using each of the following to make electricity for use in homes: sunlight, wind, coal, and nuclear reactions.

TYPE OF ENERGY	ADVANTAGE	DISADVANTAGE
Sunlight	_____	_____
Wind	_____	_____
Coal	_____	_____
Nuclear reactions	_____	_____

What are some relevant factors to consider about these methods when choosing one to make electricity for a state or country?

Factors to consider:

_____

_____

4. IDENTIFYING CAUSES AND EFFECTS

Write the missing CAUSE or EFFECT in the following table.

CAUSE	EFFECT
_____	thunder
sunlight on raindrops	_____
too much UV light	_____
too much friction	_____

5. ANALYZING DESIGNS

Why do you think a lens in reading glasses . . .

a. has curved surfaces?

_____

_____

b. is usually made of glass?

_____

_____

6. CATEGORIZING

Three things in each of the following lists are DIFFERENT in some way from the other three things. Circle the words in one group of three and explain why that group differs from the other.

oil   sunlight   wind   coal   natural gas   tides

Reason why they are different:

_____

_____

shadow   music   lens   drumbeat   ear   rays

Reason why they are different:

_____

_____

force   temperature   insulation   weight   push   boil

Reason why they are different:

_____

_____

copper   plastic   glass   iron   wood   steel

Reason why they are different:

_____

_____

7. IDENTIFYING KEY WORDS

Write down five words that have something to do with ENERGY. Add some words suggested by other people.

a. work   d._____

b._____   e._____

c._____   f._____

8. MAKING CONNECTIONS

Write a key word from question 7 at the end of each row on the following table. Then write two to six words as a connector to make a sensible sentence.

TOPIC	CONNECTOR	KEY WORD
Energy	allows our bodies to	work.
Energy	_____	_____
Energy	_____	_____

9. ASKING YOUR OWN QUESTIONS

Now ask WHY or HOW of each sentence you have made. Write down your questions and try to answer them.

Q: WHY do our bodies need energy to do work?
A: So that we can move our muscles and bones.

Q: _____
A: _____

Q: _____
A: _____

10. ASKING MORE QUESTIONS

Make up two questions about SOUND. Start your question with a word from row A followed by one from row B. Try to answer your questions.

Row A:

| What | Where/When | Which | Who | Why | How |

Row B:

| Is | Did | Can | Would | Will | Might |

Q: WHEN IS sound made?
A: When things vibrate.

Q: _____
A: _____

Q: _____
A: _____

CHAPTER 11

FOOD

Food gives us energy to move, grow, and stay healthy. Plants make their own food, but animals have to eat plants or other animals for their food supply. In some countries where there is not enough food, people spend most of their day looking for food in order to live.

Grains such as wheat, corn, and rice are used to make bread, cereals, and cakes. Vegetables and fruits come from the roots, flowers, and stems of plants. Meat comes from birds, fish, and land animals. Animals also supply us with eggs, fat, oils, and milk, which is used to make a variety of dairy products.

Sugars and starches used in making such things as cakes, candy, and bread are called carbohydrates. Fat and carbohydrates are the main sources of fuel for our bodies to burn to keep us warm and give us energy for movement.

Vitamins and minerals are important nutrients found in food. Proteins found in eggs, nuts, fish, and milk help us grow and repair any damage to our bodies.

Vitamin/Mineral	Uses
Vitamin A	fights infection, keeps skin and eyes healthy
Vitamin B	good for muscles, growing, and nerves
Vitamin C	keeps blood vessels healthy
Iron	makes red blood cells
Calcium	keeps bones and teeth healthy

1. COMPARING

Write three ways in which sugar is the SAME as salt. Both:

a. _____

b. _____

c. _____

Now write three ways in which it is DIFFERENT from salt. Only sugar:

a. _____

b. _____

c. _____

2. ANALYZING PARTS AND RELATIONSHIPS

Complete the following statements so that the last two things are related in the SAME way as the first two things.

a. Sugar is to plant as fat is to _____.

b. Cheese is to milk as candy is to _____.

c. Calcium is to teeth as iron is to _____.

3. REVERSE THINKING

List three situations in which you COULDN'T eat food.

a. _____

b. _____

c. _____

The ANSWER is food. List three questions with this answer.

a. _____

b. _____

c. _____

4. CREATIVE SIMILARITIES

List three ways in which a pair of socks is the SAME as a pizza.

a. _____

b. _____

c. _____

5. CREATIVE USES

Name four DIFFERENT uses for an apple other than as a food.

a. _____

b. _____

c. _____

d. _____

6. CREATIVE PROPOSALS

List three interesting ways of encouraging people to eat a food that they don't like.

a. _____

b. _____

c. _____

7. IDENTIFYING CAUSES AND EFFECTS

Underline the CAUSE and circle the EFFECT in the following statements:

a. Oranges contain vitamin C, which helps to keep colds away.

b. Milk comes from animals and contains calcium. This mineral helps make bones strong.

8. CATEGORIZING

Three of the following things are DIFFERENT from the others in some way. Circle them and write down WHY they are different.

apples   biscuits   nuts   potatoes   bread   wine

Reason why they are different:

_____

_____

9. IDENTIFYING KEY WORDS

Write down five words that have something to do with FOOD. Add some words suggested by other people.

a. energy   d. _____

b._____   e. _____

c._____   f. _____

10. MAKING CONNECTIONS

Write a key word from question 9 at the end of each row on the following table. Then write two to six words as a connector to make a sensible sentence.

TOPIC	CONNECTOR	KEY WORD
Food	gives our bodies	energy.
Food	_____	_____
Food	_____	_____

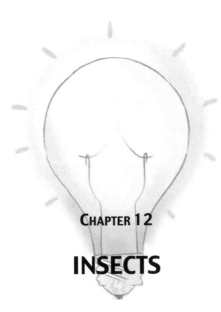

CHAPTER 12

INSECTS

Insects are small, six-legged animals. Flies, moths, and ants are just a few kinds of insects. Insects have two antennae on their heads that they use to detect odors. Their bodies consist of three segments that contain many small holes through which they breathe. Insects have wings that allow them to escape their enemies and to look for food over large distances. Fossils show that insects have survived for about 400 million years. That is because they lay hundreds of eggs and can live in freezing, cramped places. Some insects are helpful to humans because they pollinate flowering crops and produce wax and honey. Others feed on rotting plants and animals. Many insects are not as useful. These spread disease and can eat crops and timber. The life cycle of insects such as flies and butterflies is interesting because of the stages (larva, pupa, etc.) they go through to become fully developed.

1. COMPARING

Write three ways in which an insect is the SAME as a bird. Both:

a. _____

b. _____

c. _____

Now write three ways in which it is DIFFERENT from a bird. Only insects:

a. _____

b. _____

c. _____

2. ORDERING

The following things have been placed in an ORDER. What PROPERTY was used in determining this order?

birds   insects   spiders

Property used:

_____

_____

3. DISTINGUISHING FACTS FROM OPINIONS

Circle the letters in front of the two FACTS listed below:

a. Insects are not as useful to humans as birds are.

b. Insects always have six legs.

c. Insects have existed on the earth for millions of years.

d. The number of insects in the world will increase in the future.

Why are they facts?

_____

_____

4. GENERALIZING AND LOOKING FOR PATTERNS

Write down some properties or features of the following insects. If you are working with others, share your answers to create a longer list.

flies   bees   moths   ladybugs

Properties:

_____

_____

Now cross out those properties that are NOT COMMON TO ALL of your insects. Your GENERALIZATION about insects should contain only those properties that are common to all insects.

Generalization: All insects

_____

_____

5. ANALYZING DESIGNS

Why does a bee . . .

a. have six legs instead of four?

_____

_____

b. have black and yellow stripes?

_____

_____

c. have four wings instead of two?

_____

_____

6. ANALYZING PARTS AND RELATIONSHIPS

Complete the following:

a. bee is to insect as apple is to _____.
b. ant is to six as spider is to _____.
c. human is to nose as insect is to _____.

7. CREATIVE CONSEQUENCES

Complete the following sentences by placing words in the blanks.

a. If there were no more bees in the world, then _____

_____.

And this would mean that _____

_____.

8. CONSIDERING OTHER POINTS OF VIEW

Write down one reason FOR and one reason AGAINST the spraying of crops with insecticides.

For:

_____

_____

Against:

_____

_____

9. CREATIVE COMPARISONS

Would you believe that a cricket and a TV set are the SAME in many ways? Can you write down three or more SIMILARITIES?

a. _____

b. _____

c. _____

10. CREATIVE REVERSALS

Can you think of three places where you WOULDN'T find a live fly?

a. _____

b. _____

c. _____

11. CATEGORIZING

Two of the following insects are DIFFERENT from the other three. Circle them and say why they are different.

bee   moth   flea   butterfly   cockroach

Different because:

_____

_____

12. VISUAL SUMMARIZING

Fill in the missing stages and connectors in the following circular map.

BUTTERFLIES

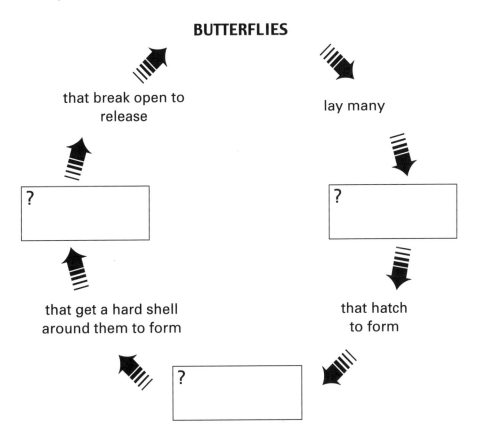

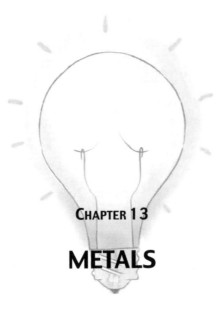

CHAPTER 13

METALS

The discovery of metals by humans allowed them to move out of the primitive Stone Age. In about 1000 B.C., some observant primitive people noticed a shiny substance, namely iron, left in the coals of their camp fires. Without knowing it, they had smelted iron ore stones with the hot carbon of their fires. This human-made metal was soon used to make knives, spears, and swords. Today we add carbon to iron to make a much stronger alloy called steel. Iron is magnetic. All metals are good conductors of heat and electricity.

The metals found on earth are mainly found combined with oxygen in the form of oxides. These are called ores. Metals such as gold, silver, and platinum are rare because they are found in small quantities in the earth as pure metals. Copper is another useful metal that is used in plumbing and electrical cables. Alloys of copper such as bronze and brass contain copper mixed with other metals. Metals can be light or heavy, strong or brittle. Over the years, scientists have discovered special properties for each metal, helping to determine how they might be used.

1. IDENTIFYING KEY WORDS

Write down five key words that have something to do with METALS. Add some words suggested by other people.

a. electricity   d._____

b._____   e._____

c._____   f._____

2. MAKING CONNECTIONS

Write a key word from question 1 at the end of each row on the following table. Then write two to six words as a connector to make a sensible sentence.

TOPIC	CONNECTOR	KEY WORD
Metals	are good conductors of	electricity.
Metals	_____	_____
Metals	_____	_____

3. ASKING YOUR OWN QUESTIONS

Now ask WHY or HOW of each sentence you made in question 2. Write down your questions and try to answer them.

Q: WHY do metals conduct electricity?
A: Electrons can pass through the atoms of metals.

Q: _____

A: _____

Q: _____

A: _____

4. COMPARING

Write two ways in which iron is the SAME as plastic. Then write two ways in which iron is DIFFERENT from plastic.

BOTH

a._____

b._____

c._____

ONLY IRON

a._____

b._____

c._____

5. ORDERING

The following stages of making iron are mixed up. Put them in the order in which they are carried out.

Purifying   crushing   mining   smelting

Correct order:

_____

6. JUDGING RELEVANCE

Write down some relevant PROPERTIES of metals that you think engineers consider when deciding on a metal to use in wires that carry electricity in our homes.

Relevant properties:

_____

_____

7. DISTINGUISHING FACTS FROM OPINIONS

Write two FACTS about iron.

a. _____

b. _____

Now write two OPINIONS about iron.

a. _____

b. _____

8. IDENTIFYING ASSUMPTIONS

People are encouraged to recycle aluminum cans. Therefore, Helen decides that aluminum must be hard to find in the ground. What is Helen assuming?

_____

_____

9. GENERALIZING AND LOOKING FOR PATTERNS

Complete the following table by writing "yes" or "no" in each cell. You may have to use a textbook to find the facts. Which properties are COMMON to all metals? What generalization can you make about metals?

Metals	Properties				
	Magnetic	Shiny	Solid	Melts Easily	Conducts Electricity
Copper					
Iron					
Mercury					
Gold					

Generalization: All metals

_____

_____

10. ANALYZING DESIGNS

Can you think of three reasons why . . .

a. coins are round?

_____

_____

b. many coins are made of a metal called nickel?

_____

_____

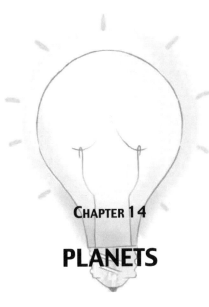

CHAPTER 14

PLANETS

The Earth is one of nine planets that circle the star we call the Sun. Some planets have satellites called moons. The Earth's Moon is important in controlling the tides of the ocean. The Earth takes 1 year to circle the Sun, while the Moon takes 1 month to circle the Earth. The table below shows more information about some of the planets.

Planets	Properties			
	Diameter (miles)	Number of moons	Days to go around Sun	Average Surface Temp (°F)
Mercury	3,050	0	88	350
Venus	7,520	0	225	860
Earth	7,930	1	365	55
Mars	4,220	2	687	−9.4

1. COMPARING

Write three ways in which the Earth is the SAME as the Moon.

Both:

a. _____

b. _____

c. _____

Now write three ways in which the Earth is DIFFERENT from the Moon. Only Earth:

a. _____

b. _____

c. _____

2. ORDERING

The following things have been placed in an ORDER. What PROPERTY was used in determining this order?

Mercury   Earth   Mars   Saturn

Property used:

_____

_____

3. DISTINGUISHING FACTS FROM OPINIONS

One of the following sentences is a FACT. Underline this fact.

a. There are more planets like Earth in outer space.

b. Mercury is an older planet than the Earth.

c. There are no living creatures on the Moon.

d. Eventually, humans will not be able to live on the Earth.

4. GENERALIZING AND LOOKING FOR PATTERNS

Complete the following table by writing "yes" or "no" in each cell. You may have to use a textbook to find the facts. Which properties are COMMON to all planets? What generalizations can you make about planets?

Planets	Properties				
	Has Moons	Has Oxygen	Is a Solid	Spins on Own Axis	Revolves Around Sun
Earth					
Saturn					
Uranus					
Venus					

Generalization: All planets

_____

_____

5. ANALYZING DESIGNS

Why are planets spherical?

_____

_____

6. ANALYZING PARTS AND RELATIONSHIPS

Complete the following statement so that the last two things are related in the SAME way as the first two things.

Earth is to planet as Sun is to _____.

7. CREATIVE CONSEQUENCES

Complete the following sentences by placing words in the blanks.

a. If the Earth no longer had a Moon, then_____

_____.

And this would mean that _____

_____.

8. REVERSE THINKING

The ANSWER is SUN. Create three questions with this answer.

a. _____

b. _____

c. _____

9. VISUAL SUMMARIZING

Write the missing words in the boxes in the following visual summary map.

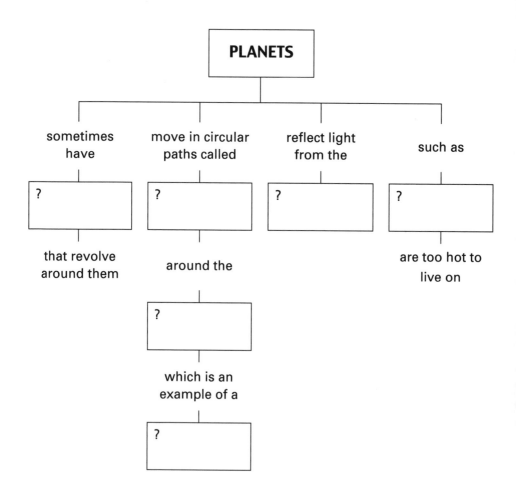

10. CHALLENGING RELIABILITY

An astronomer claims to have observed a comet whose path will cause it to hit the Earth in less than 5 years. List at least five questions you would like answered before you become concerned that the astronomer is right.

a._____   d._____

b._____   e._____

c._____

11. PREDICTING

The five planets closest to the Sun are Mercury, Venus, Earth, Mars, and Jupiter. From the table of information provided on page 117, what do you predict about the . . .

a. number of days it takes Jupiter to circle the Sun?

b. temperature on the surface of Jupiter?

c. number of moons Jupiter has?

Use a reference book to check your predictions.

12. CATEGORIZING

One of the following in each group is DIFFERENT in some way from the other three. Circle it and say WHY it is different.

GROUP   **WHY DIFFERENT?**

a. Mercury, Moon,   _____
   Venus, Mars   _____

b. Pluto, Venus,   _____
   Sun, Mars   _____

c. Earth, Venus,   _____
   Mars, Mercury   _____

13. IDENTIFYING KEY WORDS

Write down five words that have something to do with PLANETS.

a. Sun   d. _____

b. _____   e. _____

c. _____   f. _____

14. MAKING CONNECTIONS

Write a key word from question 13 at the end of each row on the following table. Then write two to six words as a connector to make a sensible sentence.

TOPIC	CONNECTOR	KEY WORD
Planets	revolve around the	Sun.
Planets	_____	_____
Planets	_____	_____

15. ASKING MORE QUESTIONS

Make up two questions about PLANETS starting with a word from row A followed by one from row B. Try to answer your questions.

Row A:

What   Where/When   Which   Who   Why   How

Row B:

Is   Did   Can   Would   Will   Might

Q: WHAT IS a planet?
A: A heavenly body that revolves around the Sun.

Q: _____

A: _____

Q: _____

A: _____

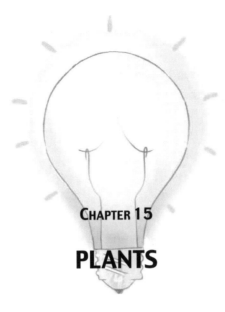

CHAPTER 15

PLANTS

Plants are living things that are fixed to the ground through roots. Consequently, they have to make their own food, which they do by converting sunlight to chemical energy (through a process called photosynthesis) and by converting carbon dioxide from the air into the oxygen animals depend on for life. Although many plants are useful to humans, each year hundreds of species of plants from the 300,000 identified are destroyed by humans in rainforests and other parts of the world. That is why many people are worried about conservation.

Giant sequoia and redwood trees are the largest of plants, while other plants can only be seen under a microscope. The cells that make up plants are very different from those that make up animals. They contain chlorophyll, a green pigment that makes photosynthesis work. Flowers are the reproductive parts of plants. They contain male stamens and female pistils. Pollen grains from the stamens fertilize the eggs in the pistil.

1. COMPARING

Write three ways in which a plant is the SAME as an animal. Both:

a. _____

b. _____

c. _____

Now write three ways in which a plant is DIFFERENT from an animal. Only plants:

a. _____

b. _____

c. _____

2. ORDERING

The following things have been placed in an ORDER. What PROPERTY was used in determining this order?

roots   trunk   branches   twigs   leaves

Property used:

_____

_____

3. JUDGING RELEVANCE

Write down two RELEVANT, or IMPORTANT, things to consider about a tree when choosing one to plant in your yard.

a. _____

b. _____

Now write two IRRELEVANT, or UNIMPORTANT, things to consider.

a. _____

b. _____

4. DISTINGUISHING FACTS FROM OPINIONS

Two of the following statements are facts. The other is an opinion. Underline the OPINION.

a. Roses are the prettiest of all the flowers.

b. Roses usually have thorns.

c. Roses exist in many different colors.

5. GENERALIZING AND LOOKING FOR PATTERNS

Write down at least three properties that all of the following trees have in COMMON.

oak   fig   eucalyptus   apple

All have

a. _____

b. _____

c. _____

Can you name any trees that don't have any of these properties?

_____

_____

6. ANALYZING PARTS AND RELATIONSHIPS

Complete the following statements so that the last two things are related in the SAME way as the first two things.

a. Plant is to sap as animal is to _____.

b. Plant is to oxygen as animal is to _____.

7. CREATIVE CONSEQUENCES

Complete the following sentences by placing words in the blanks.

a. If there were no more trees in the world, then _____

_____.

And this would mean that _____

_____.

8. CONSIDERING OTHER POINTS OF VIEW

Write down one reason FOR and one reason AGAINST allowing people in some countries to cut down thousands of trees from their rain forests.

For: _____

Against: _____

9. CREATIVE REVERSALS

Name three places where you WOULDN'T find flowers growing.

a. _____

b. _____

c. _____

10. VISUAL SUMMARIZING

Fill in the missing words and connectors in the following visual map.

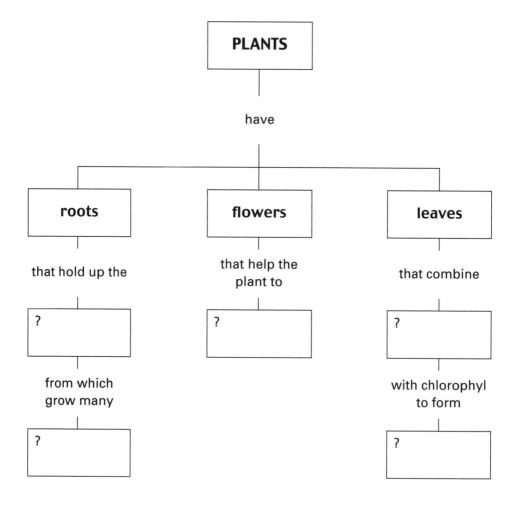

CHAPTER 16

POLLUTION

Pollution is the contamination of one substance by another so that the substance is no longer fit for its intended use. Human beings are polluting or poisoning the air, sea, rivers, and earth with gases and other chemicals. These parts of the environment have sometimes been used as dumps for disposing of unwanted substances. An example of pollution is the release of carbon dioxide from burning oil and coal products. This airborne pollutant is forming a blanket around the earth that stops heat from escaping its surface. This greenhouse effect is causing a slow melting of the ice caps at the North and South poles. One of the main ways of stopping pollution is to make laws that fine people heavily if they are found polluting.

1. IDENTIFYING KEY WORDS

Write down five words that have something to do with POLLUTION. Add some words suggested by other people.

a. oil tankers   d. _____

b. _____   e. _____

c. _____   f. _____

2. MAKING CONNECTIONS

Write a key word from question 1 at the end of each row on the following table. Then write two to six words as a connector to make a sensible sentence.

TOPIC	CONNECTOR	KEY WORD
Pollution	can be caused by	oil tankers.
Pollution	_____	_____
Pollution	_____	_____

3. ASKING YOUR OWN QUESTIONS

Now ask WHY or HOW of each sentence you made in question 2. Write down your questions and try to answer them.

Q: HOW can oil tankers cause pollution?
A: They can spill oil or flush it from their tanks into the sea.

Q: _____
A: _____

Q: _____
A: _____

4. ASKING MORE QUESTIONS

Make up two questions about POLLUTION. Start your question with a word from row A followed by one from row B. Try to answer your questions.

Row A:

What	Where/When	Which	Who	Why	How

Row B:

Is	Did	Can	Would	Will	Might

Q: WHY IS pollution bad?
A: It poisons the air, sea, and land, and it kills the animals that
live there.

Q: _____
A: _____

Q: _____
A: _____

5. CATEGORIZING

Three of the following things are DIFFERENT from the others in
some way. Circle them and say WHY they are different.

air   noise   pesticide   water   smoke   soil

They are different because _____
_____.

6. COMPARING

Write two ways in which pollution of the ocean is the SAME as
pollution of the air. Both:
a. _____
b. _____

Write two ways in which ocean pollution is DIFFERENT from air
pollution. Only ocean pollution:
a. _____
b. _____

7. GENERALIZING

List three or more typical CAUSES of pollution (i.e., pollutants). Can you see any features that are COMMON to all the pollutants you have listed?

Pollutants:

a. _____

b. _____

c. _____

Common features:

a. _____

b. _____

c. _____

8. CONSIDERING OTHER POINTS OF VIEW

Some people kill flies with flyswatters. Other people kill flies with spray insecticides. Write an ADVANTAGE and a DISADVANTAGE of killing flies in your home by each method.

METHOD	ADVANTAGE	DISADVANTAGE
a. insecticide spray	_____	_____
b. flyswatter	_____	_____

9. THINKING OF CONSEQUENCES

Complete the following sentences by placing words in the blanks:

a. If people continue to use Freon gas to squirt mists of liquids from cans, then _____

_____.

And this would mean that _____

_____.

10. IDENTIFYING ASSUMPTIONS

Tony sees many dead fish floating on top of the river in which he is fishing.

List two things he can DEFINITELY be sure of.

a. _____

b. _____

List two things he CAN'T be sure of without proof:

a. _____

b. _____

What do you think the reason is for the dead fish floating on top of the river? What evidence would you need?

My reason:

_____

_____

Evidence needed to prove it:

_____

_____

11. DISTINGUISHING FACTS FROM OPINIONS

One of the following sentences is a FACT. Underline this fact and tell why it is a fact.

a. There is more pollution today than there was 50 years ago.

b. There will be more pollution in 50 years time than there is now.

c. Young people care about pollution more than adults.

Why is this a fact?

_____

_____

12. IDENTIFYING CAUSES AND EFFECTS

Underline the CAUSE and circle the EFFECT in the following sentences:

a. There are laws to stop people from making too much noise.

b. Recycling allows us to use fewer new materials when making glass, metals, plastic, and other products.

c. The experienced pilot flew the airplane low over the fields, spraying them with insecticides. That summer very few crops were attacked by insects.

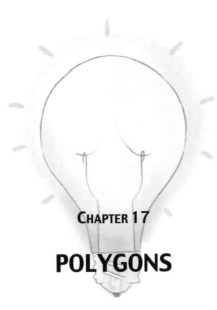

CHAPTER 17

POLYGONS

Polygons are two-dimensional geometric figures that are bound by straight lines called sides. They have a perimeter and an area. Triangles, with only three sides and three angles, are the simplest of polygons. Quadrilaterals have four sides. Some triangles and quadrilaterals have special names when they have equal sides and angles.

1. IDENTIFYING KEY WORDS

Write down five words that have something to do with PARALLELOGRAMS. Add some words suggested by other people.

a. shape   d._____

b._____   e._____

c._____   f._____

2. MAKING CONNECTIONS

Write a key word from question 1 at the end of each row on the following table. Then write two to six words as a connector to make a sensible sentence.

TOPIC	CONNECTOR	KEY WORD
A parallelogram		
A parallelogram		
A parallelogram		

3. COMPARING

Write three ways in which a square is the SAME as a circle. Both:

a. _____

b. _____

c. _____

Now write three ways in which it is DIFFERENT from a circle. Only squares:

a. _____

b. _____

c. _____

4. ORDERING

Place the following items in an ORDER. Write down what PROPERTY you used to place them in this order.

a. pentagon   triangle   square   hexagon

My order:

_____

_____

Property used:

_____

_____

b. area   side   volume

My order:

_____

_____

Property used:

_____

_____

5. CATEGORIZING

In each of the following sets of five things, two things are DIFFERENT from the others in some way. Circle them and say WHY they are different.

a. triangle   cube   square   pyramid   hexagon

Different because:

_____

_____

b. square   isosceles triangle   rectangle   pentagon   hexagon

Different because:

_____

_____

6. GENERALIZING AND LOOKING FOR PATTERNS

What properties do ALL polygons have in COMMON? Complete the table below by writing "yes" or "no" in each cell.

Polygon	Properties			
	Sides	Closed Figure	Area	Volume
Triangle				
Quadrilateral				
Pentagon				
Hexagon				

Generalization: All polygons

_____

_____ .

7. ANALYZING DESIGNS

a. Why do pencils generally have 6 sides rather than 3 or 10 sides?

_____

_____

b. Why are pipes cylindrical instead of flat-sided?

_____

_____

8. ANALYZING PARTS AND RELATIONSHIPS

Complete the following statements so that the last two things are related in the SAME way as the first two things.

a. Circle is to sphere as square is to _____.

b. Square is to four as triangle is to _____.

c. Triangle is to two as pyramid is to _____.

9. CREATING YOUR OWN QUESTIONS

A circle has a radius of 3 inches. Make up three or more questions using this information.

a. _____

b. _____

c. _____

10. VISUAL SUMMARIZING

Write the missing boxed words or connectors in the following visual map.

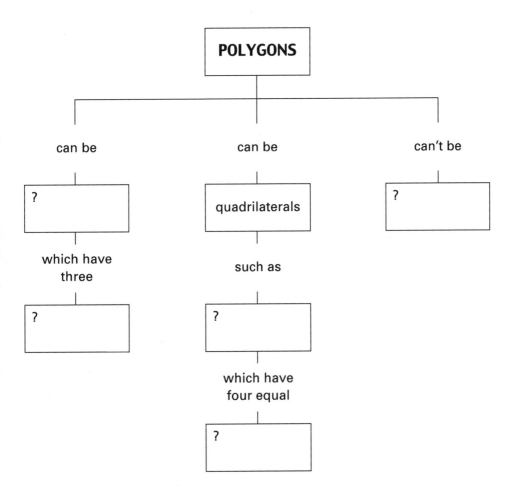

Chapter 18

WEATHER

The pressure and movement of the air, the moisture in it, and the temperature of it all combine to create our weather. Because these factors vary day by day, we rely on forecasts that predict the temperature, air pressure, and possibility of rain at different places on the earth. Weather forecasts are especially important to pilots, sailors, farmers, and other people who work outside.

Weather maps contain many symbols drawn by meteorologists that help us understand the weather in our location. The speed of moving air or wind varies widely and can result in cyclones, hurricanes, and tornadoes. The temperature of the air also varies, especially as you go farther away from the earth's surface.

1. COMPARING

Write three ways in which clouds are the SAME as lakes. Both:

a. _____

b. _____

c. _____

Now write three ways in which clouds are DIFFERENT from lakes. Only clouds:

a. _____

b. _____

c. _____

2. ORDERING

Place the following things in an ORDER. What PROPERTY did you use in determining this order?

rain   lightning   flood   thunder

My order:

_____

Reason for my order:

_____

_____

3. CATEGORIZING

Three of the following things are DIFFERENT from the others in some way. Circle them and say WHY they are different.

rain   breeze   tornado   snow   wind   fog

They are different because _____

_____.

4. DISTINGUISHING FACTS FROM OPINIONS

One of the following statements is a FACT. Underline this fact.

a. Snow is prettier to watch than rain.

b. Rain is made of the same thing as snow.

c. Snow is more dangerous to drivers than rain.

d. Air pressure is measured with a thermometer.

5. IDENTIFYING CAUSES AND EFFECTS

Write the missing CAUSES and EFFECTS in the following table.

CAUSE	EFFECT
	a rainbow
	thunder
Lack of rain	

6. CREATING DESIGNS

List some DISADVANTAGES of an umbrella.

_____

_____

What CHANGES would you make to the design to remove these disadvantages?

_____

_____

7. CREATIVE REVERSALS

Can you think of three places where you WOULDN'T find air?

a. _____

b. _____

c. _____

8. ANALYZING PARTS AND RELATIONSHIPS

Complete the following statements so that the last two things are related in the SAME way as the first two things.

a. Water is to rain as _____ is to wind.

b. Rain is to flood as lightning is to _____.

c. Thermometer is to temperature as _____ is to air pressure.

9. CREATIVE CONSEQUENCES

Complete the following sentences by placing words in the blanks.

a. If we no longer had weather forecasts, then _____

_____.

And this would mean that _____

_____.

10. VISUAL SUMMARIZING

Write the MISSING WORDS on this summary map about air.

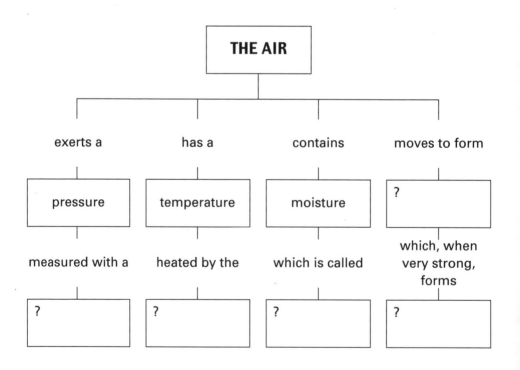

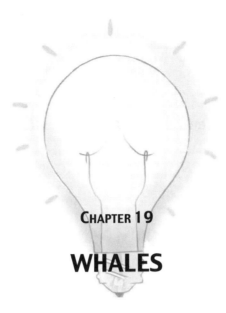

CHAPTER 19

WHALES

Although they live in the sea, whales are not fish. They are mammals that breath in air through lungs rather than gills. Blue whales are among the largest animals, growing to about 100 feet in length. Whales have big bodies but their brains are smaller than those of humans. They are, however, reasonably intelligent animals. Many whales have very large mouths but very small teeth because they feed on very small creatures called plankton. Like many birds, whales migrate to warmer waters to give birth to their young. They generally have only one calf. Different species of whales may have a life span of anywhere from 25 to 80 years or more. Humans are their only enemy, and it has been necessary to make laws to protect them.

1. COMPARING

Write three ways that a whale is the SAME as a shark. Both:

a. _____

b. _____

c. _____

Now write three ways that it is DIFFERENT from a shark. Only whales:

a. _____

b. _____

c. _____

2. CATEGORIZING

Three of these animals are DIFFERENT from the others in some way. Circle them and say WHY they are different.

whales   cows   snakes   lizards   dogs   fish

They are different because _____.

3. DISTINGUISHING FACTS FROM OPINIONS

Write down two FACTS about whales.
a. _____
b. _____

Now write two OPINIONS about whales.
a. _____
b. _____

4. ANALYZING DESIGNS

Why does a whale have such a large mouth?

_____

_____

Why don't whales generally have sharp teeth?

_____

_____

5. ANALYZING PARTS AND RELATIONSHIPS

Complete the following statements so that the last two things are related in the SAME way as the first two things.

a. Whale is to calf as cat is to _____.

b. Whale is to mammal as snake is to _____.

c. Blubber is to whale as _____ is to human.

6. CREATIVE COMPARISONS

Would you believe that a whale and a car are the SAME in many ways? Can you write down three or more reasons why?

a. _____

b. _____

c. _____

7. CHALLENGING RELIABILITY

Write down three or more QUESTIONS you would like to have answered before possibly believing a boy who claimed to have seen a white whale while fishing from a jetty.

a. _____

b. _____

c. _____

8. IDENTIFYING KEY WORDS

Write five words that have something to do with WHALES. Add some words suggested by other people.

a. migrate   d. _____

b. _____   e. _____

c. _____   f. _____

9. MAKING CONNECTIONS

Write a key word from question 10 at the end of each row on the following table. Then write two to six words as a connector to make a sensible sentence.

TOPIC	CONNECTOR	KEY WORD
Whales	swim many miles to	migrate.
Whales	_____	_____
Whales	_____	_____

10. ASKING YOUR OWN QUESTIONS

Now ask WHY or HOW of each sentence you made in question 11. Write down your questions and try to answer them.

Q: WHY do whales swim many miles to migrate?
A: To reach warm water for breeding.

Q: _____
A: _____

Q: _____
A: _____

11. ASKING MORE QUESTIONS

Make up two questions about WHALES starting with a word from row A followed by one from row B. Try to answer your questions.

Row A:

What	Where/When	Which	Who	Why	How

Row B:

Is	Did	Can	Would	Will	Might

Q: WHO MIGHT want to study whales?
A: People and scientists who study whale migration.

Q: _____
A: _____

Q: _____
A: _____

SECTION III

APPENDIXES

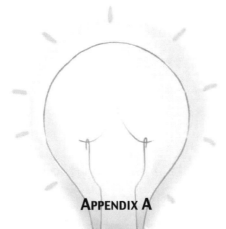

THINKING CHIPS FOR CORE THINKING PROCESSES

Here are some examples of the kinds of questions—or "thinking chips"—that good thinkers ask themselves when using the core thinking processes. These questions are meant to be used with the exercises in Section 1 of this book. Each set of questions corresponds with the Section 1 exercise that has the same bold title. If you or your classmates use other useful questions when doing a particular exercise, be sure to add these questions to the lists.

OBSERVING PROPERTIES

The acronym **SCUMPS** will help you remember the following questions. Why does this thing have this . . .
- **S**ize rather than other sizes?
- **C**olor rather than other colors?
- **U**se rather than other uses?
- **M**aterial rather than other materials?
- **P**art(s) rather than other parts?
- **S**hape rather than other shapes?

OBSERVING SIMILARITIES

- Do these things have the same **SCUMPS**—shape, color, use, material, parts, size?

OBSERVING DIFFERENCES

- Do these things have different **SCUMPS**—shape, color, use, material, parts, size?

CATEGORIZING SIMILAR THINGS

- Do these things have similar **SCUMPS**—shape, color, use, material, parts, size?

ORGANIZING THINGS IN ORDER OF SIZE

- Which thing contains all of the other things?
- Which thing is contained in all of the other things?

GENERALIZING ABOUT EXAMPLES

- Can I picture in my mind five or more examples of this thing?
- What are some parts or features of these examples?
- Can I list them?
- What parts or features are COMMON to ALL EXAMPLES on my list?

VERBAL SUMMARIZING

- What is the MAIN TOPIC or idea being discussed?
- What is the MAIN SENTENCE that summarizes what the story is about?
- Which sentences give RELEVANT information about this topic?
- Which FACTS in these relevant sentences can I use in my summary?

VISUAL SUMMARIZING

- What are the key terms in this reading?
- Are these terms connected in some geometric way?
- Are two things being compared here?
- Are three or more things being compared here?
- Are there some causes mentioned here that lead to an effect?
- Is a big thing being broken down into its smaller parts?
- Are the main and equal parts of something being described?

ANALYZING RELATIONSHIPS

- How are the first two things in the statement related?
- What fourth (missing) thing has this same relationship with the third thing?

DISTINGUISHING FACTS, NON-FACTS, AND OPINIONS

- Can this statement be proven scientifically or with evidence?
- Has this event already happened in the past?
- Does this statement contain definite words like *is, was,* and *has*?
- Does this statement contain definite numerical measurements?
- Was this statement made by a reputable authority?

DISTINGUISHING AN UNSURE CONCLUSION FROM A DIRECT OBSERVATION

- Is there observable evidence to prove my conclusion?
- Is my conclusion about feelings and beliefs?
- Is my conclusion about things that I can't see?
- Is my conclusion about things that will happen in the future?
- Am I making assumptions without evidence?

CHALLENGING THE RELIABILITY OF A CLAIM

- Did the person see, hear, or experience it first hand?
- Did anyone else see, hear, or experience it?
- Does the person have any vested interests in this thing or situation?
- How close was the person to the scene?
- Was the person in sound mind at the time?
- Is the person well respected by colleagues, friends, or classmates?
- Has the person sought publicity about this issue before?
- How experienced is the person?

DISTINGUISHING RELEVANT FROM IRRELEVANT INFORMATION

- What is your goal or main purpose?
- What features or factors are important in achieving this purpose?

THINKING CRITICALLY ABOUT WHAT YOU READ

Think of the acronym **CAMPER** to remember the following question:

- **Consequences:** What are the **c**onsequences of this belief?
- **Assumptions:** What are the **a**ssumptions being made here?
- **Main issue:** What is the **m**ain issue being discussed here?
- **Prejudice:** Is this information **p**rejudiced in any way?
- **Evidence and examples:** What is the **e**vidence to support this viewpoint? What are **e**xamples of this?
- **Reliable and relevant:** How **r**eliable and **r**elevant is this evidence or information?

Good critical thinkers are also **COOL**! That is, they try to

- **c**larify the issue and the meaning of things being considered.
- be **objective** about the issue by using facts, data, and examples.
- be **open-minded** or fair-minded by considering all viewpoints.
- be **loose** by modifying their viewpoint if they hear new facts.

MAKING A DECISION

- What is the main issue I have to make a decision about?
- What are the choices or alternatives I have to choose between?
- What are the advantages and disadvantages of each choice?
- From these, what are some relevant criteria or factors I should consider in comparing my choices?
- Can I rate or rank my choices using these criteria?
- Which choice rates the most highly overall?

IDENTIFYING CAUSES AND EFFECTS

- Which event follows after (the effect), and is directly related to another event (the cause)?

CREATIVE PROBLEM SOLVING

The first letters of the questions below spell the acronym **CREATE**:

- **Combine:** Can I combine some things in a new way?
- **Reverse:** Can I reverse some parts or processes here?
- **Eliminate:** Can I eliminate or remove some part or process?
- **Alternative:** Can I use alternative methods or materials?
- **Twist:** Can I twist things around a bit?
- **Elaborate:** Can I elaborate or add something?

Creative thinkers are also **FIRST**! They have the following characteristics:

- **Fantasize:** They fantasize or try unreal ideas.
- **Incubate:** They incubate or think about an idea for a long time.
- **Risks:** They take risks, despite what other people think.
- **Sensitive:** They are sensitive to the creativity of nature and humans.
- **Trigger:** They try to trigger new ways of thinking by being playful and having fun with ideas.

Here are more questions you might want to ask when you are thinking critically:

READING A STORY

- When and where does the story take place?
- Who is/are the main characters?
- What does the main character do?
- How does the story end?
- How did the main character feel?

UNDERSTANDING A STORY

- What does a particular word mean?
- Do I understand this sentence?
- What might be an example of this?
- Have I ever been in this situation?
- Could I teach this to someone else?
- How can I use this information?
- Why does this thing have this property?
- What are the reasons for this?
- What is the main topic here?

IDENTIFYING BIAS IN A PICTURE OR READING

- Is the group or person being shown in an unusually good or poor light (e.g., very lazy, poor, weak, dumb, glamorous, clever, strong)?
- Is an issue being presented from only one point of view?
- Is only one opinion being presented?

GENERAL PROBLEM SOLVING

- What problem do I need to solve?
- What do I have to find?
- Have I done something like this before?
- Which method did I use?
- What do I have to be careful of here?
- Can I sketch the problem?
- Can I divide the problem into parts?
- Can I use simpler numbers or parts?
- What is the first thing to do and why?
- What is the next thing to do and why?
- What will happen if I do this?
- Does this make sense?
- How am I doing?
- Have I used all of the given data?
- Does this check out?
- Is there a rule or method I should remember for next time?
- What were the difficult parts of the problem?

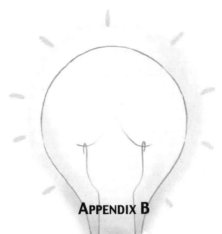

<small>APPENDIX B</small>

POSITIVE THOUGHTS TO HELP POSITIVE THINKERS

You might find it difficult to learn good thinking skills if you do not already have good emotional skills. The following thoughts will help you develop positive emotional skills.

1. CONFIDENCE

- I've done it before; I can do it again.

- Even though it may take some time, I know I can do it.

- So what if I make mistakes? Other people make mistakes.

- It doesn't have to be perfect.

- I've done difficult things before; I can do this.

- It won't be the end of the world if I can't solve this.

- I'm going to do this well.

2. PERSISTENCE

- This task may be unpleasant, but it will pay off in the future.

- I don't like it, but I will do it anyway.

<small>155</small>

- I haven't learned this yet, but I will.

- It's hard, but not impossible.

3. SELF–ESTEEM

- I am a worthwhile person because . . .

- I am not a C (or D or F) person just because I got a C grade.

- I'm good at subject X. Other people say I'm good at subject Y.

- One great thing I've done is . . .

- I can't please everyone all of the time.

- Things will be better tomorrow.

- Everyone makes mistakes. Mistakes are part of learning.

4. OVERALL POSITIVE APPROACH

- I have a supercomputer brain with more than 100 billion brain cells.

- I can learn thinking processes to improve my intelligence.

- We are all intelligent in at least one way.

- I will listen to the questions that better thinkers ask themselves when they do tasks that I can't do.

- I will learn from my mistakes.

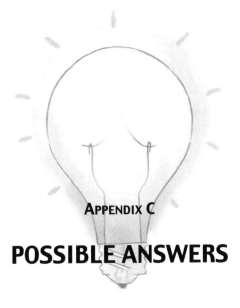

APPENDIX C

POSSIBLE ANSWERS

ANSWERS TO PRETEST OF CREATIVE THINKING (PAGES 4–5)

Possible answers for the test of creativity are listed below. Other answers are possible, but they should make sense and be acceptable to most people. The total is 24 points.

1. feelings, darkness, ideas, dinosaurs, sounds, thoughts

2. there are different types, shapes, and colors; they give off gases, take in gases, and move; they provide shelter; people can sit in them; they have many parts

3. he is hiding or blind, the inside pages are not upside down, he is asleep or shading himself

4. to build a path; as a weapon, weight, support, border, tool, or wedge; to sit or stand on; to carve; as a holder for pens/flowers; as a ruler/stencil, chalk, or a home for insects; to fill up space or lift as a weight

5. fill the pipe with water, use gum on the end of a stick, use a vacuum cleaner, or suck on a narrow pipe

6.   a shining object, fuzzy creature, measuring scale, human face, non-human face, flower, tunnel/bridge, ferris wheel, igloo/tent, arrows in a target, bush/tree, explosion, brush, half pie, ice-cream, jewelry, antennae, haystack, fallen fence, mask, slinky, pin cushion

7.

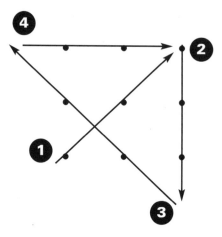

8.   Roll the sheets of newspaper into tubes. Attach a rubber band to both ends of each tube—this will stop them from unfolding. Insert the ends of the paper tubes into each other until the extended tube is 3 yards long. Place the end of the extended tube into the neck of the bottle. Roll the marble down the inside of the paper tube. You don't need to use the other things.

ANSWERS TO PRETEST OF CRITICAL THINKING (PAGES 6–9)

Possible answers for the test of critical thinking are listed below. Other answers are possible, but they should make sense and be acceptable to most people. Give a point for each correct answer. The total possible is 25 points.

1.   circle (A book is a rectangle, and a coin is a circle.)

2.   b and d

3.   e (cause); b (effect)

4.   c, d, and e

5. a: bird of prey; b: a net; c: a tree

6. every, half (price), guaranteed

7. b, e, f

8. a, d, f

9. Score a half point for each correct answer. Can be sure of: light was on, light was on in kitchen, light was on at neighbor's house, it was 3 o'clock in the morning. Can't be sure of: who left light on, why light was left on, when light was left on, if anyone was awake, if it was a mistake

10. b, e, g

ANSWERS TO WORKBOOK QUESTIONS (BEGINNING ON PAGE 12)

1. OBSERVING PROPERTIES (PAGES 12–13)

Thing	Properties	Reasons for Properties
1. brick	rough	cement sticks easily to surface
	heavy	wind won't blow it away
	rectangular	easy to stack together in lines
2. coin	round	makes it easy to handle and store
	metal	won't bend easily
	thin	light
3. flag	has colors	easy to see
	made of cloth	difficult to tear
	rectangular	easy to make
4. car tire	round	ability to roll
	rubber	flexibility
	grooved	grips the road
5. bottle	glass	easy to clean/see through
	narrow neck	easy to pour
	flat bottom	easy to stand up

6. football	made of leather	sturdy and strong
	oval shape	easy to catch and throw
	hollow	light
7. newspaper	large pages	easy to read
	made of paper	easy to print on, low cost, easy to recycle
	black print	easy to read

2. OBSERVING SIMILARITIES (PAGES 13–14)

Two Things	**Similar Properties**
1. banana and lemon	yellow, food, thick skins, grow on trees
2. triangle and square	have sides and angles, are closed and two-dimensional
3. ant and tree	living; need air, water, and sun; have internal systems
4. the numbers 4 and 9	single digits, have exact square roots, divide into 36
5. team and family	groups of people; have names, leaders, and rules
6. the words *fell* and *ran*	verbs, have one vowel, are past tense, have no capital letters

3. OBSERVING DIFFERENCES (PAGES 15–16)

Two Things	**Different Properties**
1. cat and dog	cat can climb trees, meows, chases mice
2. crab and fish	crab has claws and a hard shell, swims backward, can live out of water

3. circle and triangle   circle has no straight sides, angles, or vertices

4. lake and ocean   lake can be fresh water, is surrounded by land, has small tides

5. the numbers 4 and 11   4 is even, not a prime number, only one digit

6. newspaper and book   newspaper has low cost, is daily, has current news

7. bird and bee   bird has two legs, feathers, and bones; lives longer

8. artery and vein   artery has thick walls, carries blood from heart; arteries are fewer in number

9. verbs and nouns   verbs show action, have tenses, are fewer in number than nouns

10. president and queen   president is head of government, is elected, can be a man

11. democracy and dictatorship   democratic leaders are elected by people, allow freedom of speech and international travel, allow criticism of politicians and other powerful people, allow private ownership of media

12. the numbers 25 and 26   25 is an odd number, has an exact square root, can be divided by 5

4. CATEGORIZING SIMILAR THINGS (PAGES 16–18)

Things

Reasons They Are the Same

1. scissors, magnet, nail   made of metal, machine-made

2. ant, beetle, butterfly   insects

3. light, heat, sound — energy

4. ice, fog, steam — made of water

5. push, friction, gravity — forces

6. rabbit, deer, cow — grass-eating animals

7. coal, sunlight, uranium — can be used to produce electricity

8. lever, ramp, pulley — machines that make work easier

9. snake, alligator, lizard — reptiles

10. hydrogen, oxygen, iron — chemical elements

11. echo, music, thunder — sounds

12. election, vote, senator — involve politics

13. eating, sleeping, drinking — human needs

14. cotton, wool, hemp — natural fibers

15. photograph, page, door — rectangular

16. tire, coin, cog — round

17. cork, iceberg, apple — float on water

18. photosynthesis, shadows, photoelectricity — need light

19. the numbers 7, 11, and 13 — odd/prime numbers

20. the numbers 16, 64, and 36 — perfect squares

21. triangle, square, pentagon — polygons

22. the words *walk, catch,* and *climb* — verbs

5. IDENTIFYING NON–EXAMPLES OF A CATEGORY (PAGES 18–20)

Four Things	Different Thing	Why
1. cow, horse, dog, goat	dog	eats meat; is allowed inside
2. orange, grapefruit, pear, lemon	pear	not citrus
3. wood, plastic, cotton, rubber	plastic	not natural
4. sphere, cube, rectangle, cylinder	rectangle	not three-dimensional
5. went, smiles, climbed, sat	smiles	not past tense
6. parallelogram, square, octagon, rectangle	octagon	not four-sided
7. degrees, graphs, grams, seconds	graphs	not unit of measurement
8. Mars, Earth, Moon, Venus	Moon	not a planet
9. peninsula, gulf, cape, island	gulf	not land
10. fish, snake, bird, worm	worm	no backbone
11. president, king, mayor, governor	king	not elected by people
12. oil, timber, natural gas, coal	timber	renewable fuel
13. the numbers 12, 27, 25, and 39	25	not divided evenly by three
14. the numbers 25, 16, 21, and 36	21	no exact square root

15.

not quadrilateral

16.

not symmetrical

17. the words *run*, *rag*, *rat*, and *ram*	run	not a noun
18. the words *run*, *hit*, *slow,* and *fall*	slow	not a verb
19. oak, pine, maple, ash	pine	evergreen
20. nylon, wax, polyester, Teflon™	wax	not a plastic
21. skin, vein, hair, nail	vein	inside body
22. rat, guinea pig, mouse, anteater	anteater	couldn't have as pet
23. frost, cloud, dust, dew	dust	not a form of water
24. heat, gas, sound, light	gas	not energy
25. moon, sun, lamp, fire	moon	only reflects light
26. electron, crystal, neutron, proton	crystal	not part of atom
27. oxygen, nitrogen, carbon dioxide, hydrogen sulfide	hydrogen sulfide	not a natural gas that makes up air
28. stomach, mouth, lungs, intestine	lungs	not part of digestive system

6. COMPARING (PAGES 21–22)

Only Trees	**Both**	**Only Insects**
1. are made of wood	need air	have head and eyes
2. have roots	are made of cells	can move
3. have sap	can reproduce	lay eggs and can fly

Only Dinosaurs	**Both**	**Only Elephants**
1. are extinct	eat plants	are living
2. are reptiles	have big legs	are mammals
3. have long necks	have big bodies	don't lay eggs

Only Books	**Both**	**Only Newspapers**
1. have chapters	can have an index	can be daily
2. can have one author	are printed	include a current weather report
3. have covers	are in libraries	include current news

Only Snails	**Both**	**Only Crabs**
1. live entirely on land	have shells	can live both in water and on land
2. eat greens	hide under rocks	eat meat
3. produce slime	are living	can bite

Only Chess	**Both**	**Only Football**
1. has pieces	have players	has team members
2. is played by individuals	have rules	uses a ball
3. has a game board	have a winner	is played on a field

Only Moon	**Both**	**Only Earth**
1. revolves around the Earth	are round	has a strong gravitational pull
2. has no vegetation	have orbits	has human life
3. has no oxygen	reflect sunlight	has large oceans

7. SORTING THINGS INTO CATEGORIES (PAGES 22–24)

1. FOOD
   - Fruits: apples, berries, melons, pears, bananas
   - Vegetables: onions, potatoes, carrots
   - Dairy Foods: butter, cheese, cream, milk

2. TOOLS
   - For the Garden: spade, rake, shovel
   - For Hitting and Pounding: hammer, mallet, sledgehammer
   - For Cutting and Smoothing: plane, saw, file, sander, chisel

3. MATH CONCEPTS
   - Two-Dimensional: rectangle, foot, mile, triangle, square, kilometer, pentagon
   - Three-Dimensional: cylinder, cube, pyramid, sphere

4. BODY PARTS
   - Digestive: intestine, stomach, saliva, mouth
   - Excretory: kidney, bladder, sweat glands
   - Respiratory: nose, lungs, windpipe, mouth

5. HUMAN LIFE
   - Needs: food, water, sleep
   - Wants: car, holidays, jewelry
   - Emotions: joy, hate, jealousy

6. OCCUPATIONS
   - Media: journalist, cartoonist, actor, photographer
   - Law: lawyer, judge, prison officer, sheriff
   - Business: salesperson, manager

7. BIRDS
   - Of Prey: condor, eagle, owl, hawk
   - Water: gull, swan, flamingo, pelican
   - Flightless: ostrich, emu, kiwi

8. SUBSTANCES
   - Solid: steel, plastic, wood, copper
   - Liquid: water, alcohol, kerosene, oil
   - Gas: air, oxygen, carbon dioxide, nitrogen

8. ORGANIZING THINGS IN ORDER OF SIZE (PAGES 25–26)

1. paragraph, sentence, word
2. highway, road, lane, path
3. forest, tree, branch, twig
4. play, act, scene, speech
5. body, circulatory system, heart, artery
6. universe, sun, planet, moon

7. reflex angle, obtuse angle, right angle, acute angle
8. sensory system, eye, retina, rod
9. crystal, molecule, atom, nucleus
10. nation, community, family, daughter
11. nation, government, party, senator
12. culture, religion, Catholic, priest
13. country, state, city, suburb
14. mile, yard, foot, inch

9. ORGANIZING THINGS IN ORDER OF TIME (PAGES 26–27)

1. dawn, midday, dusk, midnight
2. lightning, thunder, rain, flood
3. egg, caterpillar, butterfly
4. bicycle, car, plane, hovercraft
5. sun, sundial, clock, watch
6. nomination, campaign, election
7. research, invent, manufacture, sell
8. compose, rehearse, perform
9. harvest, mill, bake, eat
10. design, build, paint, landscape

10. GENERALIZING ABOUT EXAMPLES (PAGES 28–32)

1. coins: are metal; have a date; are round, thin, hard
2. stamps: are issued by a country; are printed on paper; have rough edges and a value
3. English words: have letters, sound, spelling, meaning; can be part of sentence
4. polygons: have straight sides, are closed and two dimensional; have angles
5. examples: tennis, football, basketball, gymnastics, track, golf, hockey
   sports features: players, rules, winners; an umpire, referee, or score keeper
6. examples: car, bicycle, train, plane, bus
   transportation features: passenger(s), wheels, fuel, seats

7.   Some Properties of Mammals

Mammals	Properties					
	Legs	Back-bone	Lungs	Warm-Blooded	Can Swim	Can Fly
Humans	yes	yes	yes	yes	yes	no
Whales	no	yes	yes	yes	yes	no
Dogs	yes	yes	yes	yes	yes	no
Bats	yes	yes	yes	yes	no	yes

Generalization: All mammals have lungs, warm blood, and a backbone.

8. Some Properties of Metals

Metals	Properties			
	Conducts Electricity	Is Solid	Is Magnetic	Melts Easily
Iron	yes	yes	yes	no
Aluminum	yes	yes	no	yes
Tin	yes	yes	no	yes
Mercury	yes	no	no	yes

Generalization: All metals conduct electricity.

9. Some Properties of Insects

Insects	Properties				
	Six Legs	Body Segments	Antennae	Wings	Eyes
Grasshopper	*yes*	*yes*	*yes*	*yes*	*yes*
Beetle	*yes*	*yes*	*yes*	*yes*	*yes*
Fly	*yes*	*yes*	*yes*	*yes*	*yes*
Ant	*yes*	*yes*	*yes*	*maybe*	*yes*
Bee	*yes*	*yes*	*yes*	*yes*	*yes*

Generalization: All insects have six legs, segmented body parts, antennae, and eyes.

10. **Generalization:** High-fiber foods are low in sugar and low in fat.

11. VERBAL SUMMARIZING (PAGES 32–34)

Reading 1

- Possible title: We Need to Save the Great Lakes!
- Suggested main sentence: number eight, "I am amazed at the injury humans have done to the lakes . . ."
- Other relevant sentences for summary: numbers one, two, three, and nine
- Possible summary: Humans are damaging the Great Lakes. We need them for cooling cities, transport, water sports, and controlling the weather.

Reading 2

- Possible title: We Need Algae to Survive!
- Suggested main sentence: number six, "Without algae, it is doubtful . . ."
- Other relevant sentences for summary: numbers 4, 5, 7, 10, 11
- Possible summary: We need algae to survive. They make most of our oxygen and remove many pollutants in our rivers and lakes. Thousands of different algae live in all temperatures.

12. VISUAL SUMMARIZING (PAGES 34–36)

1.

Only Books	**Both**	**Only Newspapers**
a. have chapters	can have an index	can be daily
b. can have one author	are printed	include a current weather report
c. have covers	are in libraries	include current news

2. Trees have thousands of <u>leaves</u> that give off the gas called <u>oxygen</u> that is used by <u>animals.</u> Trees have many <u>roots</u> that absorb water from the <u>soil.</u> Trees <u>use</u> sunlight to combine <u>water</u> and <u>carbon dioxide.</u>

3. Butterflies lay many <u>eggs</u> that hatch to form <u>caterpillars</u> that get a hard shell around them to form <u>chrysalises</u> that break open to release butterflies.

13. ANALYZING RELATIONSHIPS (PAGES 37–38)

1. scales (Birds are covered with feathers; fish are covered with scales.)
2. bird (Blue is an example of a color; an eagle is a bird.)
3. planet (The sun is an example of a star; the earth is a planet.)
4. air (The stomach uses and absorbs food; the lungs use air.)
5. four (A triangle has three sides; a square has four sides.)
6. cube (A sphere is a solid, three-dimensional circle; a cube is a solid, three-dimensional square.)
7. courtroom (An artist works in a studio; a judge works in a courtroom.)
8. 100 (3 is 3/5 of 5; 60 is 3/5 of 100.)
9. sentence (A link is part of a chain; a word is part of a sentence.)
10. coniferous (An oak is a deciduous tree; a pine is a coniferous, or evergreen, tree.)
11. nucleus (A moon moves around a planet; an electron moves around a nucleus.)
12. electric signal (An artery carries blood; a nerve carries an electrical signal.)
13. city or town (The president governs a nation; a mayor governs a city or town.)
14. heart (The retina is part of the eye; a ventricle is part of the heart.)
15. religion (Chinese is a type of Asian race; Catholic is a type of religion.)
16. force (Heat is a type of energy; push is a type of force.)
17. rode ("Sing" is the present tense of "sang"; "ride" is the present tense of "rode.")

18. noun ("Went" is a verb; "dog" is a noun.)
19. compound (Oxygen is an element; salt is a compound.)

14. ANALYZING PATTERNS IN A SEQUENCE (PAGE 39)

1. AC (BC) CC (DC) EC (FC) <u>GC</u>
2. 2 (+ 2 =) 4 (+ 4 =) 8 (+ 8 =) <u>16</u>
3. AFGA (BFGB) CFGC (DFGD) EFGE (FFGF) <u>GFGG</u>
4. 6 (+ 3 =) 9 (+ 4 =) 13 (+ 5 =) <u>18</u>
5. 4 (+ 5 =) 9 (+ 7 =) 16 (+ 9 =) <u>25</u>
6. 24 (- 9 =) 15 (- 7 =) 8 (- 5 =) <u>3</u>

7. Dot is moving around the inside of the rectangle (from top to bottom, left to right, and bottom to top).

8. Dot is alternating from top left to bottom right corners. Square is also alternating, but from bottom right to top left corners.

9. Triangle with dot is moving around the inside of the rectangle (from top left to bottom left, bottom left to bottom right, and bottom right to top left).

10. Dot and square alternate, but remain in upper right corner. Vertical line shifts to middle of rectangle.

15. VISUALLY ANALYZING GIVEN DATA (PAGE 40–42)

1. Tom likes blue; Dominick likes orange; Juanita likes yellow; Fred likes green; Tina likes red.
2. Huang
3. Tamika
4. Mary likes water sports; Lan likes board games; Carlos likes ball games; and Bill likes gymnastics.
5. Jasmine is an accountant; Marcus is a music teacher; Derek is a computer programmer.

16 VISUALLY REPRESENTING PROPERTIES (PAGES 42–44)

1.   a. 6; b. 3; c. 5; d. 2
2.   a. 4; b. 5; c. 1; d. 1; e. 4 or 5; f. 4

17. DISTINGUISHING FACTS, NON–FACTS, AND OPINIONS (PAGES 46–47)

1. F
2. O
3. O
4. F
5. O
6. NF
7. F
8. O
9. NF
10. F
11. O
12. F
13. F

18. DISTINGUISHING AN UNSURE CONCLUSION FROM A DIRECT OBSERVATION (PAGES 48–50)

1.   Sure of: boy is holding a baseball bat, man is in chair, woman is standing, football is on man's lap.
     Can't be sure of: relationships, feelings, whose home it is, why the man is crying.

2.   Sure of: a sale at City Mart on Friday.
     Can't be sure of: *everything* and *half price* are vague. (Does *everything* mean everything out of fashion, everything damaged, and so on? Does *half price* mean half of regular price or half of the regular price after it has been doubled?)

3.   c and d

4. Possible conclusions:
   a. Switch is broken, bulb is broken, or batteries are dead.
   b. Store will be demolished, owner sold store, owner is retiring, or owner went bankrupt.
   c. World is running out of coal/oil, electricity is cheaper to make with nuclear power, or nuclear power creates less pollution.
   d. Freon causes sickness, we are running out of freon, or freon damages the atmosphere.
   e. Brand B is a better value, brand B is poorer quality, brand B is not selling too well, or brand B is bought in bulk by store.
   f. They don't reproduce easily, they are dying from a virus, they are running out of food, their habitat is being destroyed, or they have almost been hunted to extinction.

19. CHALLENGING THE RELIABILITY OF A CLAIM (PAGES 51–52)

1. Questions to ask the man who claims to have seen a dinosaur:
   - Did anyone else see it?
   - Does he have any vested interests in this? (For instance, would he make money if his story were believed?)
   - How close was he to the scene?
   - Was he of sound mind at the time? (Was he excited or tired?)
   - Is he well respected by colleagues?
   - Has he sought publicity about this issue before?
   - How experienced is he in observing and recognizing animal shapes in the wild?
   - Was he taking drugs or drinking alcohol at the time?
   - Did he report the event immediately?
   - What were the viewing conditions like at the time?

2. Believe: He had binoculars. He viewed the monster for 8 minutes. Doubt: The large gray mass was far away (1 mile from opposite shore). It had three elephant-like trunks. The man was alone. He wanted to view the monster before he died. The weather was dull and overcast with rain. He phoned the newspaper immediately.

3.   Believe: The UFO was on the ground near the car. The car was in good condition. They saw the UFO for 5 minutes. Another person saw the UFO in a nearby town. The car engine stopped as the saucer came near. Doubt: It was late at night. The family watched an air show that day. An electrical thunderstorm was in the area. The newspaper ran stories on UFOs the week before.

20. DISTINGUISHING RELEVANT FROM IRRELEVANT INFORMATION (PAGES 52-54)

1.   b, e, g
2.   c, f, g
3.   c, e, f
4.   cost, rainfall, closeness to market, soil quality, success of previous owners with crops
5.   safe (so children don't get hurt), easy to use (so children can play with toy), attractive (so children want to play with toy), interesting (so children will continue playing with toy), rugged (so toy doesn't break easily)

21. THINKING CRITICALLY ABOUT WHAT YOU READ (PAGES 54-55)

•   Words to challenge: sigh of relief, majority, ridiculous, bitter experience, problems, handful, outdated dinosaur, sure that dairy farmers don't like it, and mothers with young babies hate it.

•   Questions to ask: What is your evidence for this claim? What do you mean by "sizeable majority"? How did you sample opinions of farmers and mothers? Why do many people like daylight savings time?

22. MAKING A DECISION (PAGES 56-58)

1.   a.   How can we create an aerosol spray without using Freon?
      b.   What is another method of or fuel for propelling cars?

2.   a.   We can put trash in the ocean and in landfills, burn it, store it in old mine shafts, recycle it more often, or find ways to produce less garbage, perhaps by eliminating or reducing packaging.
      b.   We can reduce break-ins with more patrols, neighborhood watches, rewards for reporting offenders, or alarm systems.

3. a. Oil: is convenient for consumer; uses nonrenewable resource
    b. Steam: doesn't require sunlight; is expensive
    c. Solar power: is cheap and doesn't cause pollution; creates limited amount of power and requires sunlight
    d. Nuclear energy: is cheap and doesn't create smoke for pollution; poses danger of radiation leak

Questions 4, 5, and 6 have many possible answers. Make sure your answers make sense and would be acceptable to most people.

23. IDENTIFYING CAUSES AND EFFECTS (PAGES 58–59)

1. c (cause); f (effect)

2. a. The tyrannosaurus came over the hill, which caused the brontosaurus to run into the lake.
    b. The brontosaurus has a large body and small head, which caused it to eat for most of the day.

3. Sunlight causes fruit to ripen on trees. When sap stops flowing in trees, the leaves fall off. Nectar is on the flowers of plants to attract bees.

24. CONSIDERING OTHER POINTS OF VIEW (PAGES 59–60)

1. Why they shouldn't:
    a. Insecticides can poison insects and then poison the birds that eat insects.
    b. Insecticides are absorbed by crops, which are then eaten by people.

    Why they should:
    a. Insects could ruin crops.
    b. Farmers wouldn't try to grow crops for us to eat if insects would ruin them.

2. Why they shouldn't:
    a. Some types of whales will become extinct.
    b. Food that whales feed on will increase to dangerous levels.

Why they should:
a.   Some cultures depend on the meat of whales in their diet.
b.   Whaling employs people who catch whales and process their meat.

25. ASKING YOUR OWN QUESTIONS (PAGES 60–64)

Questions 1, 2, and 3 have many possible answers. Make sure your answers make sense and would be acceptable to most people.

4.   Possible math questions include:
- How much does Jack save each week? ($800 - $400 = $400; $400 ÷ 4 weeks = $100)
- What percentage of Jack's pay is used for expenses? ($400 ÷ $800 = .5, or 50%)

26. CREATIVE CONSEQUENCES (PAGES 67–68)

1.   Possible answers include:
a.   There would be more insects, so more plant leaves would be eaten.
b.   Tides would be eliminated, so the bottom of the ocean would not be stirred for fish to feed.
c.   No gasoline could be made, so cars would become useless.
d.   Some cultures would no longer be able to hunt them for food, so their native customs would be lost.

27. REVERSE CREATIVE THINKING (PAGES 68–69)

1.   You could not photograph a feeling, a sound, the universe, infinity, or the core of the earth.
2.   Open it with your mouth, hold a string placed between the pages, use a vacuum cleaner, get someone else to open it, or use some sticks or a knife and fork.
3.   He or she is hiding from someone, shading him- or herself, or is blind, or only the outside page is upside down.
4.   They both take in and give off gases, provide shade, and come in many different types, shapes, and colors.
5.   You would not find living dinosaurs, pyramids, the Eiffel Tower, or pandas in the wild.

28. CREATIVE PROBLEM SOLVING (PAGES 69–70)

1. Combine cereal and powdered milk, eliminate cardboard box and make packaging see-through, make box edible by a dog or cat, or include packaged flower seeds in the box.
2. Use gum on the bottom of a long stick, use a vacuum cleaner, or fill the pipe with water.
3.

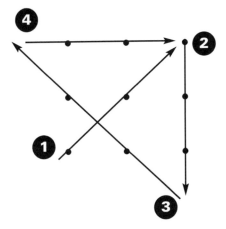

29. ANALYZING THE CREATIVITY OF DESIGNS (PAGE 71)

1. Pencils have six sides so that they are easier to hold comfortably, easier to make, and easier to pack side by side in a box.
2. Trees can't move over the ground to collect food the way animals can. They need many leaves to collect the sunlight for photosynthesis, the process that "feeds" the tree with energy.
3. Big pages are easier to read and print; fewer pages are needed in a newspaper.
4. Clay cups are cheaper and easier to make and also prevent heat loss better.
5. Dogs and cats can run faster with four legs; they need their two front legs to hold their food.
6. Red is bright and easily noticable, so it alerts you to danger quickly.

APPLYING THINKING PROCESSES TO NEW CONTENT (BEGINNING ON PAGE 73)

ANIMALS (PAGES 75–78)

1. horse, cow, rabbit: they are grass-eating, not meat-eating.
2. intelligence
3. She's assuming the bird was not killed by disease or old age, and that it didn't hit something. She'd need to see claw marks, loose feathers, and blood to prove her conclusion.
4. With four legs, it can run faster, pounce and climb more easily, and hold food.
5. Possible generalization: All animals have a head, eyes, a body, and a mouth.
6. bird; swim; bark
7. There would be more insects, more crops eaten by insects, and fewer seeds dispersed, so there would be fewer plants, flowers, and crops.
8. For: Wild elephants destroy trees.
   Against: There are limited numbers of elephants left in the world.
9. bark, speak English, and swim underwater
10. Both live in the sea and swim, and have gills and eyes.
    Only crabs have shells, legs, claws, and can live out of water.

BIRDS (PAGES 79–83)

Questions 1, 2, and 3 have many possible answers. Make sure your answers make sense and would be acceptable to most people.

4. Ordered according to their position on the food chain.
5. <u>Tommy</u> is a <u>parrot</u> with <u>black feathers</u> and a <u>yellow beak</u>.
6. Mouse: cheap to feed, but cage may have an odor. Bird: sings and is active, but needs a lot of attention to be happy. Goldfish: active and pretty, but can't be held.
   Factors: cost to feed, activity level, cleanliness
7. eagle: might eat other birds; penguin: swims in sea; hawk: has curved, sharp beak, eats mice
8. clipping its wings, building a bird house it can live in

9.

Birds	Properties					
	Has a Nest	Has Two Legs	Has a Beak	Can Fly	Lays Eggs	Eats Meat
Ostrich	yes	yes	yes	no	yes	yes
Parakeet	yes	yes	yes	yes	yes	no
Sparrow	yes	yes	yes	yes	yes	no
Eagle	yes	yes	yes	yes	yes	yes
Pigeon	yes	yes	yes	yes	yes	no

Generalization: All birds are two-legged animals that have a beak; they lay eggs and build nests.

10. For: Parrots talk; they are pretty, active, and easy to view; and they need to be fed only every couple of days.
Against: Parrots are noisy, messy, costly to feed, and they can't be handled easily. Some people think it is cruel to keep them in cages.

11. a. seeds and nuts from trees
b. fish and other animals found in or near the water
c. nectar in flowers or insects in bark
d. meat from small animals found on the ground or in trees

COMMUNICATIONS (PAGES 85–90)

1. Both are printed on paper; have indexes, a title, and authors; and are rectangular in shape. Only newspapers are printed daily, provide current news, and have fewer pages.

2. Ordered by the amount of information or number of pages.

3. b; This claim can be proved by looking in reference or text books.

4.   a.   that there is no newspaper strike, no one has stolen it, and it isn't under a bush, thrown next door, or delivered somewhere else by accident

      b.   This is the most realistic possibility.

      c.   Proof that the delivery person is sick.

5.   All media provide information, are edited, and are written by people.

6.   Yellow and black road signs are easy to see and read.

7.   There would be more jobs and calculations for humans to do, which would mean slower calculations. And this would mean that it would be harder to store and transmit information and there could be more errors.

8.   For: A person could have access to the latest information from around the world.
Against: A person could spend too much time isolated in front of the computer screen and not communicate in person with friends.

9.   underwater, in the dark, in a wind tunnel, or in a country where you don't know the language

Questions 10, 11, and 12 have many possible answers. Make sure your answers make sense and would be acceptable to most people.

DINOSAURS (PAGES 91–96)

1.   Both are large, thick-skinned, four-legged plant-eaters.
Only dinosaurs laid eggs, are extinct, and existed in many different kinds.

2.   a and d; People who study dinosaurs have documented these facts in books.

3.   She is assuming that other possible reasons, such as meteorites, diseases, and the ice age, did not kill the dinosaurs.

4.   laid eggs; had four legs and a small brain; is extinct
Megasaurus is not a dinosaur because it is not extinct—it is still alive now.

5. a.   to reach and consume leaves high in trees
    b.   eggs are easier to hide from enemies

6. birds and fish (Tyrannosaurus couldn't swim or fly.)
    Name an extinct animal. What was brontosaurus an example of?

7. a.   Large body and small head (cause) meant that the animal ate during most of the day (effect).
    b.   Approaching tyrannosaurus (cause) caused the brontosaurus to go into the lake (effect).

8. a.   Tyrannosaurus was the last to become extinct. It was a meat-eater, so it ate other dinosaurs with its sharp teeth.
    b.   size: small; food: vegetation; teeth: not sharp
    c.   had very tough skin with big blunt spikes all over its body
    d.   It ate fish because it had sharp teeth for eating meat and webbed feet for swimming.

9. They would have to be captured and kept in cages or reserves so they couldn't harm humans or other animals. And this would mean that large areas of the world would be off-limits to humans.

ENERGY (PAGES 97–101)

1. Both have waves, wavelengths, and frequencies, and are reflected. Only sound echoes and can be heard and transmitted through wires.

2. One possible ordering: heat, sound, light: in order of their speed of transmission.

3. Sunlight: It is free and clean, but costly to make electricity with (clouds and the atmosphere interfere with sunlight, so sunlight must be stored).

    Wind: It is free and clean, but not the most efficient way to make electricity (wind speed varies).

    Coal: It doesn't depend on sunshine or wind, but it is dirty and expensive, and there is a limited supply.

Nuclear reactions: It is efficient and clean, but there is a risk of radiation.

Factors: cost, pollution, availability, cleanliness

4.   Lightning causes thunder. Sunlight on raindrops causes a rainbow. Too much UV light causes sunburn. Too much friction causes heat.

5.   a. to refract or bend light rays to focus vision
      b. glass is transparent, easy to shape, and easy to clean

6.   coal, natural gas, oil: nonrenewable resources
      shadow, lens, rays: pertain to light energy
      force, weight, push: all forces
      copper, iron, steel: all metals

Questions 7, 8, 9, and 10 have many possible answers. Make sure your answers make sense and would be acceptable to most people.

FOOD (PAGES 103–106)

1.   Both are natural, crystalline, and dissolve in water.
      Only sugar is sweet, organic (from plants), and used by the body for energy.

2.   a. animal (Sugar comes from a plant; fat comes from an animal.)
      b. sugar (Cheese is made of milk; candy is made of sugar.)
      c. blood (Calcium helps build strong teeth; iron helps make blood stronger.)

3.   You couldn't eat food while scuba diving, sleeping, or singing in an opera.

      What is sugar an example of? What is burned by the body for energy? What do all animals need?

4.   Both are made by humans, sold in shops, and warm our bodies. There are different types, and they both have an odor.

5.   as a paperweight, pin cushion, ball or decoration, or to cover a hole

6. Tell the person that a person he or she admires loves to eat the food; tell the person to eat very fast; tell the person to hold his or her nose while eating.

7. a. Taking vitamin C (cause) helps to keep colds away (effect).

   b. Calcium (cause) creates strong bones (effect).

8. bread, wine, biscuits: not natural—made by humans

Questions 9 and 10 have many possible answers. Make sure your answers make sense and would be acceptable to most people.

INSECTS (PAGES 107–111)

1. Both have wings, legs, and a body, and lay eggs.
   Only insects have four wings, antennae, body segments, only one blood vessel, and six legs.

2. In order of increasing number of legs.

3. b and c; they can be verified in reference and text books.

4. Generalization: All insects have six legs, have wings, can fly, are small, and have antennae.

5. a. have more in case their fragile legs are damaged; easier to hold on and to move in cramped spaces
   b. stripes act as camouflage while they are on flowers
   c. have more in case their fragile wings are damaged; easier to maneuver

6. a. fruit (A bee is an insect; an apple is a fruit.)
   b. eight (An ant has six legs; a spider has eight legs.)
   c. antennae (A human smells with his or her nose; an insect senses with its antennae.)

7. Flowers of fruit plants would not be fertilized, so fewer fruit and vegetables would be available for us to eat.

8. For: prevents insects from eating crops
   Against: pollutes soil and air with poisonous substances

9. Both have antennae, make noise, and have a hard case.

10. underwater, in space, and in a can of insecticide

11. bee and flea: These insects can bite or sting humans.

12. Butterflies lay many <u>eggs</u> that hatch to form <u>caterpillars</u> that get a hard shell around them to form <u>chrysalises</u> that break open to release butterflies.

METALS (PAGES 113–116)

Questions 1, 2, and 3 have many possible answers. Make sure your answers make sense and would be acceptable to most people.

4. Both are solid, man-made, and molded.
   Only iron rusts, is magnetic, and is a conductor.

5. mining, crushing, smelting, purifying

6. cost, ease of forming into wire, availability, how easily a metal allows electricity to flow through it

7. Facts: Iron is an element and a conductor. It is magnetic and has a high melting point. Opinions: Iron is the most useful metal. It should always be painted.

8. Helen is assuming that aluminum is easy to make but is a hard-to-find natural resource. Actually, aluminum is an abundant element on earth that must be made into metal.

9.

Metals	Properties				
	Magnetic	Shiny	Solid	Melts Easily	Conducts Electricity
Copper	no	yes	yes	yes	yes
Iron	yes	yes	yes	no	yes
Mercury	no	yes	no	yes	yes
Gold	no	yes	yes	yes	yes

Generalization: All metals are shiny substances that conduct electricity.

10. a. They are easy to make, store, handle, and place in slots in machines.
    b. Nickel doesn't rust or wear easily.

PLANETS (PAGES 117–122)

1. Both are heated by the Sun; are round, solid, and mountainous; spin around the Sun.
   Only Earth has water, air, rivers, and living things; is a planet.

2. The planets are placed in order of their increasing distance from the Sun.

3. c

4.

Planets	Properties				
	Has Moons	Has Oxygen	Is a Solid	Spins on Own Axis	Revolves Around Sun
Earth	yes	yes	yes	yes	yes
Saturn	yes	no	yes	yes	yes
Uranus	yes	no	yes	yes	yes
Venus	no	no	yes	yes	yes

Generalization: All planets are solid bodies that spin on their own axis and revolve around the sun.

5. Because gases or molten matter are thrown into a spherical shape as they spin very rapidly.

6. star (The Earth is a planet; the Sun is a star.)

7. There would be no more moonlight and no more tides, so there would be darker nights and poor fishing conditions.

8. What is the star closest to the Earth? What allows life on Earth to exist? What is the center of our solar system?

9. Planets sometimes have <u>moons</u> that revolve around them. Planets move in circular paths called <u>orbits</u> around the <u>Sun,</u> which is an example of a <u>star</u>. Planets reflect light from the <u>Sun</u>. Planets such as <u>Mercury</u> are too hot to live on.

10. Who else saw the comet? What size telescope was used? How much experience does the astronomer have? What is the astronomer's reputation? Was the astronomer alert and awake when he saw the comet? Have other experts checked his mathematical calculations?

11. a. more days than Mars (maybe 1,000)
    b. cooler than the other planets (maybe –50°F)
    c. the same or more than Mars (maybe four)

12. a. Moon: It is not a planet.
    b. Sun: It is a star.
    c. Earth: It is the only planet that contains life.

Questions 13, 14, and 15 have many possible answers. Make sure your answers make sense and would be acceptable to most people.

PLANTS (PAGES 123–126)

1. Both are living; have cells and parts; need sun, water, air, and food. Only plants have flowers, roots, branches, and chlorophyll.

2. Property: The order in which water passes from the soil through the parts of a tree.

3. Relevant: size, cost, if it drops leaves, activity of roots, and if it is poisonous. Irrelevant: name, if other yards have them.

4. a

5. All these trees have leaves, a trunk, roots, and branches. Palm: no branches. Pine: no leaves.

6. a. blood; b. carbon dioxide

7. There would be less oxygen and more carbon dioxide, so the atmosphere would be hotter.

8. For: There would be more money for poor countries and their people. Against: Some trees would become extinct, there would be less oxygen and more carbon dioxide, so the atmosphere would be hotter.

9. at the north pole, in the dark or underground, in space (a vacuum), or in a fire

10. Plants have roots that hold up the <u>trunk</u>, from which grow many <u>branches.</u> Plants have flowers that help the plant to <u>reproduce</u>. Plants have leaves that combine <u>carbon dioxide and water</u> with chlorophyll to form <u>oxygen and starch.</u>

POLLUTION (PAGES 127–132)

Questions 1, 2, 3, and 4 have many possible answers. Make sure your answers make sense and would be acceptable to most people.

5. soil, water, and air (things that can be polluted) *or* noise, pesticide, smoke (forms of pollution)

6. Both involve chemicals, and both move over the surface of the earth. Only ocean pollution kills fish, is harder to remove, and can involve oil.

7. Pollutants: oil, insecticides, smoke, and poison
Common features: contain chemicals, used by humans, harm the environment, and are difficult to remove

8. Spray: Is quick and easy, and kills many flies, but poisons the air, stains the surroundings, and smells bad.
    Fly swatter: Is cheap and doesn't involve pollution, but can be messy, takes effort, and you can miss.

9. more Freon (propellant) would be in the air. And this would mean that the earth's ozone layer would be depleted further, letting in harmful ultraviolet rays.

10. Sure of: There are dead fish in the water. There must be a cause of death. Can't be sure of: Who or what caused the deaths? When? Why and where?
    Possible reason: There was a lack of oxygen because of too much algae in the water.
    Evidence needed: Algae in the water; tests showing low oxygen content in the water.

11. a. We have evidence to prove it; increased population has caused increased pollution.

12. a. Laws (cause) reduce noise (effect).
    b. Recycling (cause) reduces the need for new materials (effect).
    c. Insecticide (cause) reduced insect attacks (effect).

POLYGONS (PAGES 133–137)

Questions 1 and 2 have many possible answers. Make sure your answers make sense and would be acceptable to most people.

3. Both are two-dimensional closed figures with a perimeter and a center. Only squares have straight lines, angles, and corners.

4. a.   triangle, square, pentagon, hexagon: ordered by number of sides
    b.   side, area, volume: ordered by number of dimensions

5. a.   cube and pyramid: three-dimensional
    b.   isosceles triangle and rectangle: all sides not equal

6.

Polygon	Properties			
	Sides	Closed Figure	Area	Volume
Triangle	*yes*	*yes*	*yes*	*no*
Quadrilateral	*yes*	*yes*	*yes*	*no*
Pentagon	*yes*	*yes*	*yes*	*no*
Hexagon	*yes*	*yes*	*yes*	*no*

Generalization: All polygons are closed figures that have sides and an area.

7. a. Six sides make them easier to hold, make, and pack together.
    b. The round shape is much stronger and less likely to fracture.

8. a. cube (A sphere is a three-dimensional circle; a cube is a three-dimensional square.)
    b. three (A square has four sides and corners; a triangle has three sides and corners.)
    c. three (A triangle is two-dimensional; a pyramid is three-dimensional.)

9. What is its diameter? What is its area? What is its circumference?

10. Polygons can be <u>triangles,</u> which have three <u>sides.</u> Polygons can be quadrilaterals such as <u>squares,</u> which have four equal <u>sides.</u> Polygons can't be <u>circles.</u>

WEATHER (PAGES 139–142)

1. Both contain water, are sometimes odd shapes, and move in the wind. Only clouds don't have a shore line, don't have tides, and float in the sky.

2. Lightning, thunder, rain, flood; this is the natural sequence in which these events would occur.

3. wind, tornado, breeze (all are moving air) *or* rain, snow, fog (all are forms of water)

4. b

5. Sunlight on raindrops causes a rainbow. Lightning causes thunder. A lack of rain causes crops to die.

6. Disadvantages: spokes break, material tears, and water comes in from the sides.
    Changes: make flexible spokes, use a stronger material, and make the umbrella larger.

7. in space, in a vacuum, and on a planet such as Venus

8. a. air (Rain is made of water; wind is made of air.)
    b. thunder (Rain causes a flood; lightning causes thunder.)
    c. barometer (A thermometer measures temperature; a barometer measures pressure.)

9. We wouldn't know if, when, and where it would rain or storm, so people could be caught outside in severe storms and there would be more plane and boat accidents.

10. The air exerts a pressure measured with a <u>barometer</u>. The air has a temperature heated by the <u>Sun.</u> The air contains moisture, which is called <u>water vapor.</u> The air moves to form <u>wind,</u> which, when very strong, forms <u>tornadoes or hurricanes.</u>

WHALES (PAGES 143–146)

1. Both live in the sea; swim; have a tail, skin, and eyes.
    Only whales have lungs, blubber, and warm blood.

2. whales, cows, dogs: all are mammals.

3. Facts: whales are mammals; they migrate.
    Opinions: Whales are nicer than sharks; no one should kill them.

4. They have large mouths to take in large volumes of water containing small plankton, a source of food. The teeth of some whales are not sharp because they don't eat meat; they filter the plankton in their large mouths.

5. a. kitten; b. reptile; c. fat

6. Both move long distances, have a streamlined shape, and make noise.

7. Did anyone else see it? How far away was it? Have you ever seen one before? Did you use binoculars? Do you have good eyesight? Have you ever reported such an incident before?

Questions 8, 9, 10, and 11 have many possible answers. Make sure your answers make sense and would be acceptable to most people.

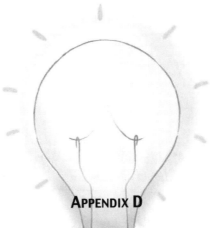

REFERENCES AND ADDITIONAL RESOURCES

BOOKS AND ARTICLES

Barell, J. (1995). *Teaching for thoughtfulness: Classroom strategies to enhance intellectual development* (2nd ed.). Reading, MA: Addison Wesley.

Bellanca, J., & Fogarty, R. (1993). *Catch them thinking: A handbook of classroom strategies Grade 4–12.* Arlington Heights, IL: Skylight.

Beyer, B. (1987). *Practical strategies for the teaching of thinking.* Boston: Allyn and Bacon.

Burke, K. A. (1993). *The mindful school: How to assess thoughtful outcomes.* Arlington Heights, IL: Skylight.

Campbell, L., Campbell. B., & Dickinson, D. (1998). *Teaching and learning through multiple intelligences* (2nd ed.). Seattle, WA: New Horizons for Learning.

Costa, A. L. (1991). *The school as a home for the mind: A collection of articles.* Arlington Heights, IL: Skylight.

De Bono, E. (1975). *CoRT thinking.* Oxford, England: Permagon Press.

De Bono, E. (1992). *Serious creativity: Using the power of lateral thinking to create new ideas.* London: HarperCollins.

De Bono, E. (1999). *Six thinking hats.* Boston: Little, Brown.

Fogarty, R., & Belanca, J. (1989). *Patterns for thinking: Patterns for transfer.* Arlington Heights, IL: Skylight.

Gardner, H. (1993). *Frames of mind: The theory of multiple intelligences* (10th annual ed.). New York: Basic Books.

Lazear, D. (1992). *Teaching for multiple intelligences.* Bloomington, IN: Phi Delta Kappa.

Lazear, D. (1999). *Eight ways of knowing: Teaching for multiple intelligences: A handbook of techniques for expanding intelligence.* Arlington Heights, IL: Skylight.

Marzano, R. J. (1988). *Dimensions of thinking: A framework for curriculum and instruction.* Alexandria, VA: Association for Supervision and Curriculum Development.

Paul, R. W. (1992). *Critical thinking: What every person needs to know in a rapidly changing world.* Santa Rosa, CA: Foundation for Critical Thinking.

Perkins, D. N. (1986). *Knowledge as design.* Hillsdale, NJ: Lawrence Erlbaum Associates.

Perkins, D. N. (1992). *Smart schools: From training memories to educating minds.* New York: Free Press.

Presseisen, B. Z. (1990). *Learning and thinking styles: Classroom interaction.* Washington, DC: National Education Association.

Resnick, L. B. (1989). *Toward the thinking curriculum: Current cognitive research: 1989 ASCD Yearbook.* Alexandria, VA: Association for Supervision and Curriculum Development.

Swartz, R. J., & Parks, S. (1994). *Infusing critical and creative thinking into content instruction: A lesson design handbook for the elementary grades.* Pacific Grove, CA: Critical Thinking Press and Software.

Wang, M. C., Haertel, G. D., Walberg, H. J. (1994, January). What helps students learn? *Educational Leadership, 51*(4), 74–79.

Wiederhold, C. (1991). *Cooperative learning and critical thinking: The Question Matrix.* San Juan Capistrano, CA: Resources for Teachers.

Wiggins, G. (1989, April). Teaching to the authentic test. *Educational Leadership, 46*(7), 41–47.

Wiggins, G. (1992, May). Creating tests worth taking. *Educational Leadership, 49*(8), 26–33.

Young, G. (1973, August). Is It Too Late? *National Geographic, 144*(2), 147–185.

Zahl, P. (1974, March). Algae: The life-givers. *National Geographic, 145*(3), 361–377.

WEB SITES

- Edward De Bono's Website: www.edwdebono.com

- National Center for Creativity: www.creativesparks.org

- Sonoma State University Center for Critical Thinking: www.criticalthinking.org

For more web sites, use a search engine to search under the following terms: *thinking+creativity* or *critical+teaching*.

ABOUT THE AUTHOR

JOHN LANGREHR, PH.D., is an Australian who has taught in American and Australian high schools. His teaching career also includes more than 25 years as a cognitive psychologist at the University of South Australia. Dr. Langrehr received his Ph.D. in cognitive psychology and education from Ohio State University.

For the past 15 years he has followed the growth of interest, particularly among American educational institutions, in developing student thinking processes. He has also taken an active role in providing materials to help educators develop student thinking, through publications, conferences, and consulting. He has written 12 books (three published by NES) and more than 50 articles on the topic of improving student thinking processes.

Dr. Langrehr has been an invited speaker at the annual Critical Thinking Conference at Sonoma State University, California, at the National Schools Conference Institute Conference in Phoenix, Arizona, and at national conferences on thinking and gifted education throughout Australia. As a government consultant, he has spoken to thousands of Australian teachers involved with helping students develop their intellectual potential. He presently lives in Australia, where he works as an educational consultant.

Teaching Our Children to Think emphasizes Dr. Langrehr's belief that we have to help all students learn to ask better questions to probe the ever-growing amount of information available to them. He believes that one way to do this is to encourage thinkers to reflect on and share the kinds of patterns they sense in information, the mental pictures they use to summarize it, and the "unconscious" key questions they ask themselves when doing specific mental or physical tasks. This conscious reflection on and sharing of thought processes is called metacognition. Research shows that regular use of metacognition in the classroom is a powerful factor in improving student learning.

Teaching Our Children to Think focuses on more than 25 of the core thinking processes that students can use every day to make sense of information. The second part of the book allows students to apply these core thinking processes to a range of high-interest topics.

About *Teaching Our Children to Think* and the National Educational Service

The mission of the National Educational Service is to provide tested and proven resources that help those who work with youth create safe and caring schools, agencies, and communities where all children succeed. *Teaching Our Children to Think* is just one of many resources and staff development opportunities NES provides that focus on building a community circle of caring. If you have any questions, comments, articles, manuscripts, or youth art you would like us to consider for publication, please contact us at the address below. Or visit our website at:

www.nesonline.com

Staff Development Opportunities Include:

Improving Schools Through Quality Leadership
Integrating Technology Effectively
Creating Professional Learning Communities
Building Cultural Bridges
Discipline With Dignity
Ensuring Safe Schools
Managing Disruptive Behavior
Reclaiming Youth at Risk
Working With Today's Families

National Educational Service
304 W. Kirkwood Avenue, Suite 2
Bloomington, IN 47404-5132
(812) 336-7700
(800) 733-6786 (toll-free number)
FAX (812) 336-7790
e-mail: nes@nesonline.com
www.nesonline.com

NEED MORE COPIES OR ADDITIONAL RESOURCES ON THIS TOPIC?

Need more copies of this book? Want your own copy? Need additional resources on this topic? If so, you can order additional materials by using this form or by calling us toll free at (800) 733-6786 or (812) 336-7700. Or you can order by FAX at (812) 336-7790, or visit our website at www.nesonline.com.

Title	Price*	Quantity	Total
Teaching Our Children to Think	$24.95		
Adventure Education for the Classroom Community	$89.00		
As Tough as Necessary: Discipline with Dignity (video)	$395.00		
Developing Literacy and Workplace Skills: Teaching for the 21st Century	$159.00		
Gifted Learners, K–12	$19.95		
Professional Learning Communities at Work (book)	$24.95		
Professional Learning Communities at Work (video)	$495.00		
The Balancing Act: A Multiple Intelligences Approach to Curriculum, Instruction, and Assessment (video)	$395.00		
What Do I Do When . . . ? How to Achieve Discipline with Dignity	$21.95		
		SUBTOTAL	
		SHIPPING	
Continental U.S.: Please add 5% of order total. Outside continental U.S.: Please add 7% of order total.			
		HANDLING	
Continental U.S.: Please add $3. Outside continental U.S.: Please add $5.			
		TOTAL (U.S. funds)	

*Price subject to change without notice.

❑ Check enclosed ❑ Purchase order enclosed
❑ Money order ❑ VISA, MasterCard, Discover, or American Express (circle one)

Credit Card No._____ Exp. Date_____
Cardholder Signature _____

SHIP TO:
First Name_____ Last Name_____
Position _____
Institution Name_____
Address_____
City_____ State_____ ZIP_____
Phone_____ FAX_____
E-mail _____

National Educational Service
304 W. Kirkwood Avenue, Suite 2
Bloomington, IN 47404-5132
(812) 336-7700 • (800) 733-6786 (toll-free number)
FAX (812) 336-7790
e-mail: nes@nesonline.com • www.nesonline.com